THE DARK SIDE
OF JAPAN

ALSO BY ANTONY CUMMINS

THE DARK SIDE OF JAPAN

ANCIENT BLACK MAGIC, FOLKLORE, RITUAL

ANTONY CUMMINS

AMBERLEY

First published 2017

Amberley Publishing
The Hill, Stroud
Gloucestershire, GL5 4EP

www.amberley-books.com

Copyright © Antony Cummins, 2017

The right of Antony Cummins to be identified
as the Author of this work has been asserted
in accordance with the Copyrights, Designs
and Patents Act 1988.

ISBN 978 1 4456 6302 9 (paperback)
ISBN 978 1 4456 6303 6 (ebook)

British Library Cataloguing in Publication Data.
A catalogue record for this book is available
from the British Library.

Typesetting and Origination by Amberley Publishing
Printed in the UK.

Western civilisation has invaded all this primitive peace with its webs of steel, with its ways of iron – the old gods are dying!

Lafcadio Hearn

CONTENTS

ACKNOWLEDGEMENTS

Most translations are by Yoshie Minami and she must be thanked for her continued support and guidance; also Mieko Koizumi, who worked on translating the spells from the *Zoho Majinai Chohoki Daizen* document. I am grateful to Gabriel Rossa for his help with the esoteric and to Jackie Sheffield for her help with the first run-through of the text. Finally, a big thank you to David Osborne for his superb illustrations.

INTRODUCTION: WELCOME TO HELL

The Japanese – who are they? Or rather, who are they to those in the West? The masters of paper folding and car production, faceless salarymen, computer nerds and tourists machine-gunning the world with their cameras? For the generations before the war and Japan's subsequent climb to economic success, the Japanese were a mysterious people; they inhabited mountains hidden by deep mists. They were a people of esoteric teachings, some aficionados of ancient ceremonies, others masters of warfare, clad in their strange armour and steeped in bloodthirsty ways. Their image was rooted firmly in the medieval and was more or less created by the Victorians. This culture, isolated from the Industrial Revolution, represented a richness that we had lost through the progress of technology. Indeed, Japan is surely unique in having once rejected a key instrument of modern technology, having given up the gun and reverted to the sword in the seventeenth century. Bearing in mind that Japan probably had more guns than any other country in the world at this time, to eliminate them almost entirely was an extraordinary achievement by the nation's samurai class. But we intruded on Japan as a hidden enemy, threatening to destroy its culture. While Japan is still a cultural goldmine, it has been stripped by tourism and trade with the West and is starting to look played out.

At first Japan seems to be alive with tradition, but after years of living among the Japanese I can see the cracks beginning to show. Japan sells out its own past, and the corporate types will flog anything 'Japanese' while we Westerners lap up the deception. In truth, when you work your way into Japanese society, it becomes clear that most Japanese have almost no idea what Japan was before the arrival of the West, in the same way as we only have a vague and media-defined understanding of our own medieval traditions. To find true beauty and culture in Japan you have to seek out real masters and faithful artisans who have a firm grasp on their particular tradition and art. It is these people who hold the threads of the old ways in their hands, but generation by generation these threads are being let loose. My aim here, if possible, is to refresh the mystery. I am searching for new avenues to rediscover the phenomenal attraction the world felt for Japan. In this volume I want to take you along the river of Hell, through cities of the damned and into the heart of all that is dark in Japanese folklore. Here I hope you will find a reminder of that distant, terrifying and beautiful land.

Pulling out the Pages

Imagine me deep in a vast castle archive or in a Japanese monastery, tearing the pages from ancient manuscripts, whispering dark spells and bringing forth images of Hell, making deals with demons and pacts with the Devil during my research. Well, no, that's not actually what happened; it was something less dramatic. Normally, I am a part of a small team that searches out and discovers ancient ninja and samurai manuals and we bring these to an English-speaking audience. At times I find myself waiting on my two trusted translators, as their part in our work takes considerably longer than mine. Thus, with time and energy to spare I began to probe for an independent project I could work on that would not create too much work for my translators. It was at this point I began to re-read some of Lafcadio Hearn's work on the supernatural. Hearn (1850–

1904), who is known in Japan as Koizumi Yakumo, was of Irish-Greek descent and spent much time in Japan. He became famous for collecting Japanese folklore and ghost stories. Reading through his work I was impressed again by the immense amount of information he had collected, but at the same time I found myself trying to bypass his Victorian travel writing. His descriptive approach is totally understandable for his day, but now there is no need for page upon page of description or commentary about the Japanese people; we can get it all on Google.

So the idea came to me. I could rediscover all those who in the Victorian era and slightly beyond recorded Japanese folklore and myths, and then preserve the 'essence' while peeling off the Victorian redundancies. This led me on a library hunt to discover

The old John Rylands Library on Deansgate in Manchester, the special collections branch of the University of Manchester, where I collected much of the information for this book. (Courtesy of Michael D. Beckwith under Creative Commons)

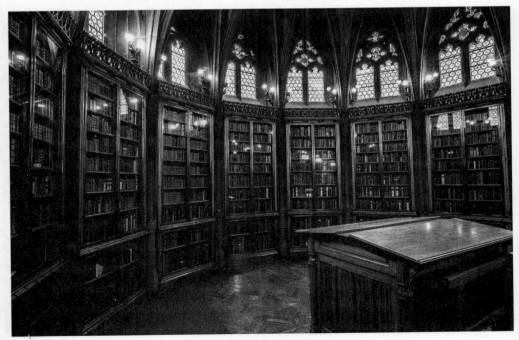

writers who from the end of the nineteenth century up until the 1950s had spent their time recording the legends of the East. A record of Japanese beliefs began to emerge, which I began to arrange for a modern audience. This has led to many parts being stripped down and overly complex cultural undercurrents being removed. During this marshalling of the material came the natural development of three categories: the hellish, the heavenly and the downright curious. This volume will concentrate on all the maleficent elements of Japanese folklore.

I have kept the spelling, names and place names the same as in the original works. However, I have removed all diacritical marks.

Finally, it must be remembered that these stories and legends come from all over Japan and across centuries, and therefore what was known in one area may have been unknown in another, or what was thought at one time was rejected or forgotten later. So when venturing into the dark mists of Japanese folklore, you will not always have a firm grasp of time and location.

Mixing and Matching

One aspect of Japanese culture that is difficult for the Western mind to grasp is the ability to *integrate*. With no doctrine of monotheism and no banishment of other religions, Japan has been a relatively open place for religion and custom. Of course Japan had its times of religious persecution and conflict, but no single religion ever won out for long. This has resulted in Shinto ceremonies, Buddhist funerals, Christian weddings and shamanic rituals existing happily side by side. This eclectic mix does not faze the Japanese, and nor should it faze you. From an academic standpoint you could dissect the entire contents of this book and attribute sections to Buddhism, Shinto, Confucianism, Taoism, the magic of *Onmyodo*, and more. Why bother? This was not an issue for the people of historical Japan, nor is it an issue in Japan today. Two further points distinguish East from

West. First, as Professor John Gray writes in his extraordinary and controversial book *Straw Dogs: Thoughts on Humans and Other Animals*, 'A feature of the idea of modernity is that the future of mankind is always taken to be secular ... In China and Japan, where the Judeo-Christian and Islamic idea of religion has never been accepted, secularism is practically meaningless.' Second, as author Roland Kelts points out concerning Japanese culture both today and in history:

> You only have to look to the Japanese language for insight. Common words such as *ganbaru* (to slog on tenaciously through tough times), *gaman* (enduring with patience, dignity and respect) and *jishuku* (restraining yourself according to other's needs) convey a culture rooted in pragmatism and perseverance. (*New Statesman*, March 2015)

Chinese Connections

A question that is almost impossible to answer is, 'Just what is Japanese?' Japan and things Japanese are familiar to us all, but in truth those Japanese elements are in many cases imported. India, China and Korea have all had some influence on Japan in the past, and much of Japanese culture found its way to the islands through Chinese connections. This means that when studying Japanese systems and ways you can almost always see some hint of China in the shadow, some echo of the Asian mainland. With this in mind, do not become confused when China keeps popping up like a dragon from the ocean, and understand that many of the elements in this book can also be found in Chinese folklore.

BEASTS, ANIMALS AND CREATURES

The line between that which is supernatural and that which is imbued with supernatural powers is thin in Japan, but it can still be drawn. This first chapter will take you into the wilderness and investigate the native creatures of Japan and the hellish reputation they have for supernatural powers and acts of mischief.

Foxes, Raccoons, Badgers and Dogs

Racoons and foxes are considered to have magical powers in Japan. It is considered in ancient folklore that these creatures can morph into human shape or hide as objects, goblins or other animals and that when they reach 1,000 years old they turn gold or white and sport nine tails. An ancient Japanese saying tells us of the powers of transmutation that these creatures had:

狐の七化け狸の八化け

(Foxes can mutate in seven ways, while raccoons can mutate in eight)

Foxes were so powerful in the Japanese imagination that it is believed one ruler of Japan, Lord Hideyoshi, wrote a letter to the god of foxes asking the fox-king to stop one of his servants from possessing one of Hideoyshi's servants and respectfully warning that if the god of foxes did not cooperate then Hideyoshi would kill every fox in the land.

These creatures are also seen as tricky spirits who can possess you. Some Japanese witches (for want of a better term) would try to gain control over a fox to attach themselves to it, using it as a familiar. To gain a firm hold over a fox-spirit you should do the following:

1. Find a pregnant vixen.
2. Tame the vixen.
3. Once tame, help her as she gives birth to the fox cubs.
4. The vixen will then ask you to name one of her cubs.
5. Once named, the cub is bound to you and will carry out your demands as a familiar.

Possession by fox is called *kitsune-tsuki*, while possession by dog is called *inu-tsuki* or *inu-gami-mouchi*. In the Oki Islands, dog possession was more common than fox possession. This was once a very real issue to the Japanese, and those accused of possession by a dog or fox in Japan could be exiled from their villages and their families could be ruined. Foxes that possess a woman curse the family, for once a family had a fox reputation then its members were not allowed to marry into other families that did not have the same affliction. There appears to have been genuine persecution of those thought to be the victim of fox possession. It was also known as 'fox-ownership', and there was a set of regulations controlling the interaction of families who had such fox-ownership.

A trick for avoiding demon foxes: if you are walking down a road at night and there is a 'man' sitting on the corner with a long snout, with a scarf over his head who may be dressed as a priest and is beating out a rhythm on his belly or scrotum – but

yet appears to not be in pain – do not approach him because he is a fox or racoon spirit. There is even a 'dance of the fox', called *kistune odori*.

It is said that the spirit of a fox could pass on from female to female in each human generation, and these females came to be known as witches and their families were harassed. As late as 1922 there were reports of Japanese witches (including males) using the spirits of foxes to possess people to do them harm or even to kill.

One story of a badger: a badger of ill intent stole the food of a man who, upon seeing that it had been stolen by the creature, captured the badger and tied it up to his roof beams. While the wife was preparing food and the man was out in the woods, the badger took the voice of a human and spoke to the woman, saying that he would make amends by helping her to prepare the food. Untying the creature was her last mistake; it killed her and took over the food preparation, chopping her into the meal. The badger now transformed itself into the image of the wife, and when the man returned home the 'wife' fed him this grisly meal.

One tale talks of flying dogs: a pupil named Shujushi saw two dogs magically leap over a great ravine and so went to find his master, Genshin. They both crossed to the other side and found a plant there, which they dug up. It had roots shaped like dogs, so the two boiled the roots and made a magic powder out of them that gave them both the power to fly.

Wolves

The *Tenshin Katori Shinto Ryu* sword school of Japan has bushcraft from the fifteenth century that involves wolves: when in the woods and confronted by wolves you should hold a stick above your head, vertical and high. A wolf will not attack anything that it cannot jump over, thus hold the stick high and the wolf will not attack.

A story that has been passed down describes wolves who once put out a fire that woodsmen left alight within the forest. The wolf pack ran down to the river, submerged themselves and then went back to the fire and dowsed the flames.

Hares

The hare (remember it is not a rabbit) is associated with the moon in Japan, and it is said that they can live for an extremely long time. Between the ages of 500 and 1,000, a hare will turn pure white. Hares are generally good creatures, and one even helped to kill the evil badger in the story above; he did this by disguising himself and tricking the creature who had just fed the man his own wife. The hare is known to live on the moon, pounding away on a pestle and mortar, making the elixir of life. The hare is also a main character in the stories of the White Hare of Inaba and Kadzutoyo and the Badger.

Cats

It is said that when Buddha died only the venomous serpent and the cat did not weep, and therefore the cat was once seen as malignant. A cat is said to be full of witchcraft and capable of changing into a woman, be it an old crone or a seductive singing girl who will put you under a spell. On the other hand, Japanese sailors prize cats for their ability to keep the spirits of the deep at bay; a cat of three colours is deemed best. A sailor feels that anyone who has drowned at sea is restless, and the white crests of waves on the shore are the hands of the dead, clawing up the beach; the cat is thought to control them.

The 'vampire cat' is one such story about the evil will of the feline. Once there was a prince of Hizen who had a lover called O-toyo, whom he adored. One night O-toyo awoke to a giant cat in her room, which seized her and strangled her. It then hid the body and transformed into the guise of O-toyo herself. The prince, not seeing through the disguise, loved her as much as ever. However, little by little his health began to fail and eventually his officers saw the need for vigilance.

Some 100 faithful samurai were stationed in his room to guard over him at night, but each night they all fell asleep and his state worsened. Night after night they could not remain awake, and no one knew the reason why. Ruiten, a priest, was called but again to no avail. One night, while the priest was getting ready for the night vigil, he saw a samurai washing himself and praying to Buddha. This samurai was Ito Soda, and he was too low in rank to talk directly to the lord but wished to serve as best he could. The next day it was decided that the young Ito Soda could remain with the lord and his 100 samurai at arms. Sleep came over the company, but Ito Soda had placed oiled paper down on the floor and stabbed himself in the leg whenever he felt sleep coming, twisting the knife to keep him awake. After a while the door opened, and in came

the cat disguised as O-toyo. She smiled to see everyone asleep, but spotted the conscious Ito Soda and faked concern for the prince. The next morning the lord felt revived, and the next night the same happened again. Ito Soda could fight the magic of the cat. He told people of his experience, and they believed him as the prince was acquiring power and health again. So, under the pretext of being a messenger, he knocked on the fake O-toyo's door and she answered. The samurai said to her, 'Read the message.' As she did so he lunged with his dagger, but she fended him off and reached for a halberd and met him in combat. The woman-cat, being outmatched by the samurai and the eight knights waiting for her outside, turned back into a cat and escaped. She ran into the mountains, where the prince led a hunting party and killed her.

The following is another tale, this one of a mountain cat spirit. One day a young samurai knight took shelter in a temple, where he intended to spend the night. Just before midnight there came to him the illusion of a dancing and shrieking troop of cats, who cried out, 'Tell it not to Shippeitara', at which point the cats faded away. The next day the samurai enquired in the village and found out that Shippeitara was a great dog belonging to a vassal of the prince. He also discovered that one of the young maidens of the village was to be sent in a cage to a mountain spirit to be used as a human sacrifice. The samurai took it upon himself to free the maiden – in classic chivalric form – and secured the use of the great dog Shippeitara. The samurai placed the dog in the cage instead of the maiden and travelled to the mountains. The men who had helped get the cage with the dog to the appointed place ran away, and only the bold samurai remained. At the appointed time came the troop of cats as expected, but this time they were accompanied by a giant tomcat who was the incarnation of the evil mountain spirit. The knight waited for his moment, and as the great cat was laughing in anticipation of devouring another maiden the samurai opened the cage and the powerful dog attacked the feline leader, taking it in his jaws and giving the samurai time to kill the evil creature. The dog then made short work of the other cats, and the village was jubilant at the success of the adventure.

It was considered by some extremely terrible to kill a cat, as they were magical creatures; to kill one would bring bad luck for seven generations. To prevent this seven-generation curse, certain measures could be taken.

In Okinawa they would hang the dead body of the cat from a tree or bury the cat at a crossroads where three or four roads intersect. On the Ryukyu island chain (an arc from Kyushu to Taiwan including Okinawa), if you kill a cat with a car, the car will be haunted by the cat's dead spirit. To counter this, bury the cat at the edge of the town with cooked rice, bean paste and salt. On the same islands, cats are sometimes eaten for medicinal purposes.

In Akita, if a cat or dog dies you should spit on it three times and walk around the corpse three times to dispel the bad luck;

if you do not do this, the spirit of the animal will haunt you. Alternatively, you can leave the corpse in a bamboo forest.

If someone is born in a year of the Snake, a cat will not stay with them.

If a black cat crosses your path, move backwards sixteen steps, or you will be cursed.

If you leave a cat with a dead body, the body will dance.

Pigeons
An old shamanic tradition states that if a pigeon enters your house and flies to the east on leaving, all is well – it may even mean you are about to go on a journey overseas. If it flies to the west and then lands in a graveyard, someone will die.

Crows
An ancient shinobi poem tells us of crows (all 100 poems can be found in *Secret Traditions of the Shinobi*):

かど出にからすの声のきこゆるは　はんなるぞよきちやうはつつ
しめ

(When you leave home, if you hear a crow call an odd number of
calls, it is lucky [for your mission]. Thus, an even number suggests
that you should be careful)

Additionally, unmarried girls should avoid eye contact with crows.

Butterflies
A fluttering butterfly, meandering its way into a room between the paper-lined sliding doors could, according to tradition and to Hearn, be inhabited by a soul from the realm of the dead. These beauties could be harbingers of death; it is said that when the rebel samurai Taira no Masakado was about to revolt a host of butterflies flew

into the streets of Kyoto, where it was taken as an indication of the numbers who were about to die. Tradition holds that the soul of a person can become, or enter, the butterfly *before* death. The soul of a dying person may occupy or form the shape of a butterfly to declare its intention to leave the land of the living. More positively, if a butterfly lands within the guest room of the house, the person that you most love will be arriving shortly. The butterfly can also identify the position of an enemy so that vengeance may be achieved.

Mosquitoes

Like the butterfly above, the mosquito has connections with those who have passed to the other side. These tiny creatures can be the reincarnation of a human, brought back to the world as a tiny pest, sentenced to drink blood due to transgressions in a previous life; people so afflicted are known as *jiki ketsu gaki*, which is a form of blood-drinking creature.

Ants

In Taisu in old China there was a man who worshipped a goddess, day in and day out. One day while at worship a woman in a yellow robe came to him and said she was the goddess he was so devoted to. She rewarded him for his service by letting him understand the language of ants. From her golden robe she pulled out a box which contained an ointment. The goddess dabbed this ointment on his ears and told him to find some ants and stoop down to them and listen. He began to venture off but came across some ants before he had even left the threshold of his house. Bending down, he listened to them. At once he heard them talking and their conversation was of treasure. One ant said to another, 'Let us move on from this cold and damp place as the buried treasure here will not let the sun heat the soil.' Hearing this, the man got a spade and found jars of treasure, making him rich – but never again did he hear the language of ants.

Even up until relatively modern times, hotels would put up signs which demanded that ants should pay a fee for using a room. Because ants do not like to open their wallets, they see the sign and do not enter the hotel.

Wasps

At Todaiji temple, it is said that wasps are meant to issue forth from the mouth of a statue at times of war.

Dragons

Japanese dragons are essentially from China, but one difference is that a Japanese dragon normally has three claws while the Chinese counterpart has five. Dragons are associated with water, seas, lakes and rivers, being more connected with water than with fire. However, the dragon can sometimes breathe fire or even rain, and has the ability to ascend into heaven or turn invisible. There is a legend that tells of a dragon from Yamashiro that would transform into a howling white bird called O-goncho every fifty years. When the bird came, so did great famine.

Birds

In Japan the dove can be seen as a messenger of war, having saved the life of the shogun Yorimoto. Also, a bird called Hototogisu is said to be able to travel in the land of the dead.

2

THE DEAD AND HUMAN SACRIFICE

The afterlife in Japan is based on a mixture of religions including native Shinto and Buddhism. The Japanese see the dead as not moving away but instead taking up the role of *kami* – minor deities who stay within the area and even become involved in the lives of humans.

The very ancient Japanese, upon finding a dead relative in the house, would abandon the house and live elsewhere. They would leave the body of the relative where it lay and offer up food and drink, light a fire outside the house and perform music and dance and hold rituals for a period of eight to fourteen days. After this they would bury the body and allow the house to become a shrine. Alternatively, a small mock house was built for the recently deceased to live in.

There is also a very old and horrific custom for the dead; this is the *hitogaki*, or 'human hedge', and involves human sacrifice. They would bury alive a number of humans in a circle around the burial place of one who has died (who was of course higher-ranking). These sacrifices were buried upright with only their heads left exposed, where they would cry and lament for the recently dead, and after a time they would die as animals would eat at their faces and heads. Allegedly, this practice was stopped around 2,000 years ago by the Emperor Suinin. However, it appears to have continued until the sixth century, when the Emperor Kotoku again forbids self-strangulation, the strangulation of others, the stabbing of thighs and voluntary suicide at the graves of the recently dead. It has been postulated that this rite never died out and that it simply changed to the act of *seppuku*, ritual suicide by disembowelment by sword, known in the west as *hari-kari* (spelt correctly *hari-kiri*). This version of *seppuku* was known as *junshi*, which is to follow the lord to the afterlife in service and was not a punishment but an honour.

An older form of human sacrifice is talked about by Hadland-Davies. If the image of a bow appeared above a house, it meant that the eldest daughter was to be sacrificed by being buried alive so that the wild beasts had something to devour; this would promote good hunting.

Another tale of human sacrifice comes from a castle in Matsue, where it is said a nameless girl who loved dancing was killed and put beneath the walls to placate the old gods. If any woman or child dances in the street then the castle shakes with her rage.

One custom for burying the dead was to hang a *sanyabukkero* purse around the neck of the dead with three copper coins in it (three *rin*) so that they could pay to cross the River of Three Roads, which is known as Sanzu no Kawa. In Izumo, the price was six *rin* and the river was called Rokudokawa – the River of Six Roads. The parallels with the River Styx are unmistakable (and it should be remembered that 'Styx' translates as hate or detestation – no Christian paradise here).

The Death Tablet

This is a lacquered death tablet, a small wooden slat that has a base and stands vertically. It has the posthumous death name of the dead upon it so that the family can remember their departed, sometimes as a minor god. It has to be remembered that to the Japanese a dead relative becomes an ancestor ghost/god who needs to be nourished with food. The dead take the

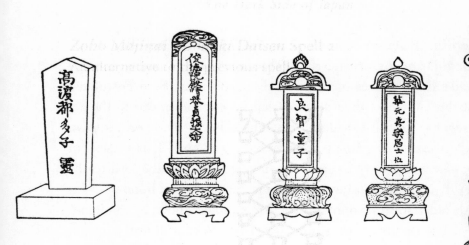

Various Japanese death tablets.

invisible essence of the food and become involved with family dealings, haunting the death tablets and generally staying around the family to protect and disturb the realm of the living. In short, the dead do not fade away as in Western tradition; they become powerful, controlling human affairs and nature, and therefore need to be placated.

Hair for the Dead

The hairstyle for a woman who has died and is being prepared for her funeral is called *tabanegami*, which must also be worn by women who are in a period of mourning. However, ghosts are mainly shown with their hair loose and flowing. Hearn states that in Japanese culture a woman's hair is her most prized asset and to give it up is extremely difficult. A samurai who did not wish to kill his wife after she had transgressed in some way could cut off her hair and throw her out; equally, if a samurai died and his widow pledged to never see another man she would cut off all of her hair and place it in the coffin on his knees, never to let it grow again. However, most would take just one lock of hair, placing it with the dead as a token of respect.

3

HAGS, VAMPIRES, GHOULS
AND GHOSTS

Japan has more than its fair share of weird and malignant creatures. This section will give a short introduction to some of the basic kinds, plus their powers and skills and the evils they commit. The subject is so vast that this introduction must not be seen as comprehensive. One word that will always crop up when looking at these creatures is *yokai*, a generic term to mean 'monsters'. However, while *yokai* is becoming more and more familiar as a term, it has not always been a catch-all description. In medieval Japan, the term *bakemono* referred to numerous creatures although it specifically means 'changeling', something which transforms its shape (and is solid). The more childish or adolescent version of this is *obake*, used in children's conversation, but if you really wish to impress you can use the more academic term *kaii gensho*. Whichever terms you use, you should remember that Japan was once a collection of disparate areas, sometimes lacking fixed boundaries and a unified vocabulary. Ideas and stories were not consistent, changing from place to place and from time to time.

Ghosts
In short, there are two types of ghosts. The first is *shi-ryo*, which is the spirit of someone who is dead. These only haunt at night. The second is *iki-ryo*, which is the spirit of a living person. The

Japanese believed that if someone was angry enough their spirit, without them knowing it, could leave the body and attack their enemy in broad daylight. This second version is more fearful than the first as it wishes to kill. The most famous version of this is Lady Rokujo in the epic tale *Genji Monogatari*.

A rule of thumb for Japanese ghosts: *bakemono* implies a solid creature, while *yurei* implies an ethereal creature.

Tama or *Tamashi* are said to be ghosts in the form of pearl-like orbs, which could be considered as souls. They leave the body upon death and move to the next stage of existence.

'Yoshitsune attacked by Taira spirits' by Utagawa Kuniyoshi, 1853. The general defeated the Taira clan in the late 12th century. (Courtesy of the Rijksmuseum)

Kappa

Kappa are small, goblin-like creatures that have the body of a child, the face of a tiger (adorned with a beak) and the shell of a turtle and/or the scales of a fish. They dwell in rivers and ponds and wait for people to pass by so that they can drag them in and drown them. Interestingly, the *kappa* also kills humans by removing a fictional organ from the body via the anus. On the top of a *kappa*'s head you will find an indent which is filled with water. It is said that if this dries up or empties then the *kappa* will become powerless.

In the legends of Tono (discussed later), if a woman gives birth to a *kappa* baby after being raped, or if a *kappa* baby is born generations after the original copulation, then the baby is to be taken outside and hacked to death.

Tengu

The *tengu*, 'heavenly-dogs', are considered to be long-nosed goblins or demi-demons; they can also come in a form known as *karasu-tengu* that is half man and half crow. They are said to dwell in the mountains and are mischievous and sometimes evil. It is claimed that they teach martial arts and endow warriors with mystical powers. At times, *tengu* will even kidnap children. Their leader is Dai-tengu, the Great Goblin, who rules above them holding a seven-feathered fan. It is thought that *tengu* broke the laws of the Buddha and therefore belong neither to heaven nor to hell. Lane, in his early twentieth-century book on legends, tells us that the famed swordsman Miyamoto Musashi killed a *tengu*, which is no mean feat as *tengu* are considered expert swordsmen.

One story of a *tengu* is as follows. Some boys were tormenting a bird and an old man passed by and saved the bird from dying. As he went on his way a mountain hermit came to him and thanked him, declaring that he was the bird he had saved. The traveller knew that instant that he was talking to a *tengu*. The *tengu* offered him supernatural powers in reward but the man said he had no need of them and his only wish was to see the original Buddha giving a sermon. The *tengu* said he could transport him through time and space and show him such a thing, but that the man must say nothing and remain silent at all times. The man agreed, and the *tengu* took him to Vulture Mountain back in the time of the Buddha. There he saw hosts of spirits and demons and holy men listing to the Buddha. Unable to control himself, he cried out in reverence and that instant was transported back to his original position and to face a very angry *tengu*, who had his wings broken as punishment. The *tengu* scolded the man and was never seen again.

Sometimes *tengu* steal people and return them in a demented state; this is referred to as *tengu-kakushi*, or being 'hidden by a Tengu'. One example of this is Kiuchi, a samurai who went missing; his fellows came upon his equipment strewn around and in the end found him on a temple roof, at which point he told his story. He said that he had met with a black-robed monk and a larger man with a red face. They had told him that he must climb onto the temple roof, and when he refused they broke his sword and scabbard and carried him to the roof. There they made him sit on a tray, and through magic they made the tray float; it took him through the skies to many regions across the land. After ten days of this, Kiuchi prayed to Buddha. The tray then landed on a mountain, but the mountain turned into the roof of the temple where he had begun.

Demons and Devils

Demons are known as *oni* in Japanese and devils are *akuma*. However the translation of these terms is not always straightforward. The horned *oni* is more of an ogre for a Western mind: large, lumbering at times, normally of a strange skin colour and armed with a massive club. Normally *oni* patrol hell and do evil – as you would expect of a demon – but some *oni* are known to cut off their horns and try to become monks, as the horn of an *oni* is its weakness and power. These good demons study under a human master to find enlightenment. In the main, though, *oni* are evil and work in hell. Some small *oni* may be found tickling a monk's head, trying to disturb him from his meditation. There is even an island of *oni* called Onigashima.

Shojo

These creatures live near the coast and are monkey-like in appearance. They have red hair which can grow long on their heads and they are said to party hard on the seashore and get very drunk. (Surely one of the earliest examples of discrimination against redheads.) If you capture one you can make a great dye from its hair, so fishermen try to capture them to make a profit.

Goryo

Goryo, sometimes *goryi-shin*, are the malevolent spirits of once noble humans who died in political intrigue. They create epidemics, disasters and even wars. Their infamy and the fear they produced was so vast that even the emperor of Japan used to lead ceremonies to appease them, the first such ceremony taking place in Kyoto in 863. Later on in Japanese history, a *goryo* could be made from the soul of a lower-class person; they simply had to ardently will themselves to become this destructive god on their deathbed. In fact, it is thought in Japanese culture that even a lifetime of positivity can be washed away by a negative mindset in a person when they are about to die. *Nembutsu*, which is the recitation of the name of Buddha, is said to drive them away or to quell their power.

A point of interest is that *nembutsu* ascetics would go to extreme levels to prove their willpower and devotion. It is said that they would flay the skin from their palms and the sides of their feet or hold their hands in fire, even amputating their own fingers and toes to test their willpower. However, most extreme of all was their practice of public suicide. They would announce their intention to either hang, drown or burn themselves. Crowds would then gather to watch, and reports even came of beautiful music or coloured clouds appearing as enlightened ones came to take the now dead devotee to paradise. While this may not be the best afternoon pastime, if you had a *goryo* devil after you then these *nembutsu* practitioners were the guys you needed to help you out.

Another element of *nembutsu* was the *nembutsu odori* – the *nembutsu* dance. Practitioners would dance in a large circle around an altar, banging on drums and playing musical instruments, all to rid the area of *goryo* spirits. Interestingly, it has been theorised that the modern *bon-odori* dance for the dead – the now famous festival in which people dance around a village platform – is based on this ancient magical practice.

Yuki-onna

Yuki-onna, or 'the lady of the snow', is a beautiful 'vampiric' female who has pure white skin, raven-black hair and blood-red lips. She is thought of as a snowstorm incarnate and is noted for her evil doings, trapping travellers in the snow, blowing down doors, tricking parents to their deaths as they search for lost children and killing with her icy breath. In one tale she falls in love and marries, although with sad consequences.

The area of Tono also has a 'snow woman'; however, the translator, Morse, did not include the original Japanese ideograms in his work and so it is unknown if this is the same figure. Perhaps one of the saddest, if not the most fearful of the many stories of the *Yuki-onna* describes her holding a child in a blizzard. She asks passers-by to hug the child. If one does, the child becomes heavier and heavier and the Good Samaritan, covered by the snow, freezes to death. (See *Ubume*, page 39.)

Medusa
In Japanese folklore, it is thought that a woman's hair can quite literally turn into snakes. There are men who see a woman's reflection in a mirror and observe that the hair in the reflection is full of snakes. Moreover, there are tales of men who see the hair of their otherwise friendly wives and concubines turn into snakes that try to bite the lady opposite, their reflections showing their true feelings towards one another.

Tsukumogami
It is believed that when an object reaches 100 years old it has the ability to become animated. These animated objects are iconic in Japanese culture: kettle stands with arms and legs, teapots running around the house, and so on. The name is believed to be a play on words, as it implies and sounds like the number ninety-nine (that is, next year it will animate itself). The last word is *gami*, or hair, in this case grey and old. Keep an eye on those antique books on your shelves!

Gyokushi
This is a being that has the power to call forth the storms and the wind and rain to petrify crops and grasses and to build castles from dust.

Kazane no Enkon
This unfortunate woman was killed by her husband with a farming sickle and turned into a vengeful spirit. She is often portrayed with a round face and one eye closed while the other is open. The closed eye has come to represent the moon, the open eye the sun.

Ubume

This mysterious hag waits on the side of the road with a baby in her arms. She asks passers-by to take the baby for a moment while she attends to some need or other. The kind-hearted soul who helps her is left with the baby in arms. Little by little the baby gets heavier and heavier until the person is pulled to the floor, the duress too much; when they look to see that the infant is alright they discover it has turned into a boulder.

Raiju

This is said to be a small creature that falls from the sky when there is a lightning storm. It is like a cat or a monkey, and if you take the bark of a tree which it has scratched, then the bark can ease toothache.

Kishimonji

The mother of demons is a hag who in life continually involved herself in cannibalism, eating many children. In some versions of the story, the original Buddha gave her a pomegranate to eat as it was close to the texture of human flesh. The end of her tale differs depending on which version you read. In one form she is sent to hell to give birth to many children to replace the ones she devoured – apparently 500 children in total. The other version states that she is sent to hell to become the mother of demons, giving birth to demon after demon to repay her debt. In most stories, however, she become enlightened and joins Buddha.

Mitsume

This 'beautiful' hag is extra-special in her grotesque appearance. Seated on a chestnut horse, she has three eyes and elongated teeth that are 4 inches long. Blue in colour, she wears the flayed skin of dead men and her horse's girdle is made of snakes. She trots along on human bones, drinking human blood from a skull.

Mikoshi Nyudo

If you are getting changed behind a screen, then be careful when you look upwards! The *mikoshi nyudo* is a creature that has a bald head and a lolling tongue. It looks over Japanese screens at people getting changed, scaring them.

Nukekubi

This is a creature that has the power to take off its head and have the head move around on its own, normally for evil intent.

Rokurokubi

Similar to the above is the *rokurokubi*, a creature of the same ilk that, instead of detaching its head, extends its neck great lengths.

Ashinaga and *Tenaga*

Ashinaga have long legs while *tenaga* have long arms. They share a connection to fishing.

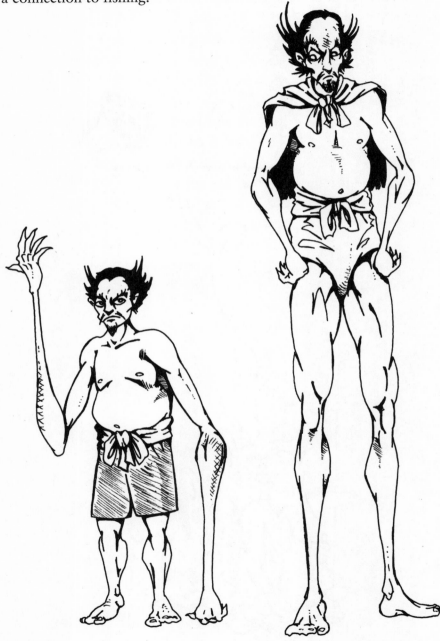

Human Heads on Mythical Creatures

The following examples are strange incarnations of human faces and heads on mythical creatures.

Shokuin	A red dragon said to be 100 *ri* (almost 250 miles) long with a horned human face; its breath produces storms.
Shinriku	A tiger that has a human head. However, this human head has eight smaller human heads on its crown.
Soriushi	A snake with nine human heads.
Sahoku no Shinjin	A large dog with a human head.
Hotai	A monkey with a human head.
Teishin	A fish with a human head.
Takujiu	A creature with six horns, two on its human head and four on its back. It has a bearded face, hairy legs, an ox tail and three eyes on each flank.
Umi bozu	This is a tortoise with a human head.

4

SPIRITUAL DAYS IN THE JAPANESE CALENDAR

A major part of medieval Japanese life was the yearly calendar, comprised as it was of festivals, rituals and special days. Included in these are some of the darker aspects of magical times, such as days which are connected with the afterlife or have ominous meanings. It is beneficial to understand that Japan based its calendar on a Chinese system that drew from both the solar cycle and the lunar month. For ease, all dates or days are shown in lunar months as this is the best English translation; however, that being said, there was a complex system to line up both the solar and lunar calendars. Remember the first month is not January. To understand when the first month is, simply look up the date of the Chinese New Year for the year in which you read this.

Obon: The Festival of the Dead

This traditionally occurs on the fifteenth day of the seventh month of the lunar calendar, when the moon is full, which means that the date changes each year in modern terms. (More recently, however, since the adoption of the Gregorian calendar, the date has moved to the fifteenth of either July or August depending on the region of Japan.) It is believed that the dead walk among the living during this short period of time, and Japanese people celebrate with a traditional dance called *bon-odori*. They light the outsides of their homes and float small lanterns on rivers to help guide the dead back to the spirit realm. The term *hotoke-umi* is used in connection with this and means 'tide of the returning ghosts'. If a real ship is caught in the middle of the river lanterns, then the ghosts call out for buckets from the sailors, but the sailors only give them bottomless buckets so that they cannot use them to sink the ship.

Hearn states that one possible origin story for this dance of the dead was that when a man gained the Six Supernatural Powers of Buddhism, one of them gave him the ability to see his mother in the afterlife; seeing her hungry, he left food for her dead spirit. However, when she picked up the food it turned to hot coals and burnt her mouth and fingers. He sought advice and was told that on a specific day he should leave food for all the dead priests of all the world and not just his mother. Following the instructions, he gave food for all the dead and they ate it with glee. His mother, being so happy, 'danced for joy'.

The dead are sometimes said to inhabit mountain areas, and in some parts of Japan it was the custom during this festival to hike to a mountaintop and use fires to attract their attention. Once you had the attention of the dead, you would lead them down the mountainside and into your house. It has been recorded in Japanese tales that a wife may prostrate herself at the doorway to welcome the dead and ask forgiveness for the lack of bounty or the poor quality of the home, regardless of how much there actually was to eat and drink.

When the festival is over, small lanterns bearing the family name are paraded to a nearby river and set afloat, allowing the dead to follow their family names to the afterlife with ease.

To make a floating lamp, choose wood that floats and cut a square 10 inches by 10 inches and at the corners put four 10-inch-long stanchion-posts which are connected at the top by slats of wood. Next, drive a nail upwards from underneath so that a candle can be attached. The sides should be filled in with coloured paper, these colours representing the five elements: side 1, red; side 2, blue; side 3, yellow; side 4, the right side of the paper, black; side 4, the left side of the paper, white.

Alternatively there are *shoryobune*, which are straw Chinese boats in the style of junks. These are up to 4 feet long and have the names of the dead written on white cloth sails. On the mini deck is a cup of water and incense for the dead. Banners painted with a swastika are tied to the rigging.

Boichi is the market of the dead; this was a market set up just before *obon* to sell things concerning the dead and things that would be needed for the festival. This market would continue up to the dance of the dead itself.

At *obon* people are not allowed to eat fish for the period of the festival. Additionally, if both of your parents are alive then the first time you can eat fish again is on the sixteenth day of the seventh lunar month; if you have lost one parent then you have to wait until the seventeenth to start eating it again.

Hearn says that when geisha lose a 'sister' they set up mats and a table in a temple. With the death tablet of the girl before them, they play their instruments and perform for free.

Setsubun: The Bean-throwing Festival

Setsubun literally means 'division of the seasons', and the festival would traditionally happen as each season changed into the next. However, this festival has come to be practised once a year on the third of February. The aim is to dispel evil from your home and to invite luck into the household. It is common for a family member to dress as a demon by wearing a mask and for the rest of the family to throw roasted soya beans from inside the house to the 'demon' outside while chanting, '*Oni wa soto! Fuku wa uchi!*' ('Demons leave – luck please enter.')

Tangono Seku: The Feast of the Iris

On 5 May you should spread scented iris petals around your garden. This is done to scare away any demons or evil spirits.

Chishigo: The Tides and Times of Death

In ancient Japan there was a belief that you could predict when people were going to die, or at least understand the times at which people were more likely to move on to the next life. This method was constructed around the tides and the hours of the day. The Days of Death are as follows:

On days of the lunar months which end in 1st, 2nd, 9th, 10th, 20th or 30th, people will die in the hours of the Ox, the Dragon, the Ram and the Dog.

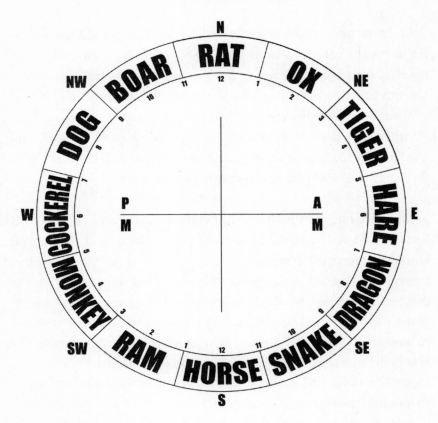

On days of the lunar month which end in 6th, 7th or 8th, people will die in the hours of the Tiger, the Snake, the Monkey and the Boar.

Surprisingly, this system appears to not cover the days where the number of the day ends in 3rd, 4th or 5th, this could either mean that it was believed that no one died in this period of time or that part of this system is lost to us. If the latter is the case it would mean that people would die on days ending in 3rd, 4th or 5th in the hours of the Horse, the Hare, the Cock and the Rat.

Unlucky Days

In ancient times in Japan there was the concept of *fujōnichi*, or unlucky days; it is on these days that you should not ask others anything as it is a negative time. The days and times are as follows and are based on the lunar calendar:

Date of the Month	Duration
1st	All day
4th	At night
8th	Daytime
18th	At night
25th	Daytime
29th	At night

The Coming-of-Age Ritual

Coming of age, that is surviving puberty and moving to adulthood, is a ritual found in all cultures throughout history. In Japan this can be divided into two basic forms: the upper-class ritual of *ui koboshi* or *kakan*, which involves a special form of headdress; and the lower-class ritual of *gen buki* or *eboshi iwai*, which is a copied form of the former, again utilising a headdress. The subject's name will often be changed at this point, and women may dye their teeth and have facial tattoos or tattoos on the backs of their hands (this only occurs in some places and is rare). However, what we are interested in here is the darker side, and some of these rituals included a journey to a misty mountain where the youth was led through the mists by one of the infamous Yamabushi priests to return as a part of the adult community.

Ill-fated Years

Some years in Japan are considered positive while some are considered negative; in fact, according to Japanese tradition your age itself can have a positive or negative connotation. One old superstition is that a woman born in the combination year of *hinoe* and horse – which comes around every sixty years – will have a husband that will die young. Not an attractive pointer for any would-be suitors!

5

BASIC JAPANESE MAGIC

Japanese 'magic' is not really a single coherent art, and nor does it have identifiable boundaries. Varying across the land, it encompasses divination, exorcism, ritual magic, animal and human sacrifice, spirit worship and more.

In Japanese magic, there are eight elements that give power to the curses and spells that are cast:

1. Nailing or stabbing a spell into an object.
2. Imitating the action of shooting or cutting.
3. Burning.
4. Binding or wrapping.
5. Stepping on an object.
6. Tying.
7. Ceremoniously opening objects.
8. Using containers with no bottom, which represent the womb.

Words of Power
In Eastern and Japanese magic there are words of power, and each falls into one of three categories. They are used variously to provoke suffering, to provide protection and to help in difficult circumstances.

1 Words of Power with Meaning

The first category for words of power are those words with a meaning; that is, they are understood by the speaker. You are to use these words when you are in dire peril, for instance if you are lost at sea, in a fire or surrounded by bandits. Example words are:

Kanzeon	A deity of mercy
Bosatsu	An enlightened one
Fumombon	A scripture to the deity Kanzeon Bosatsu

2 Words of Power without Meaning

The second category are words of power that were once Sanskrit but that have been changed over the years and have lost their original meaning. That is, they are no longer sound like their Sanskrit ancestor. These are said to have the power to relieve suffering when spoken out loud. Some words are:

Abira Uken Bazara dato ban
On amiritateizei karaun
Nama samman da basaranan

After saying these above three lines the caster should repeat the heart sutra below:

Gate gate paragate parasamgate bodhi svaha (Sanskrit)
Gyate gyate haragyate haragyate bochi sowaka (Japanese)

3 The Names of Gods

The third and final category for words of power concerns the names of gods; these are used to give the speaker power or aid them in their quest. The names of the gods are spoken out loud and with force (to be repeated three times). The mantra is as follows:

Hagorosan Daigonden, Hagorosan Daigonden, Hagorosan Daigonden.

Gassan Daigonden, Gassan Daigonden, Gassan Daigonden.

Yudonosan Daigonden, Yudonosan Daigonden, Yudonosan Daigonden.

Arasawa emmei jizo daibutsu, Arasawa emmei jizo daibutsu, Arasawa emmei jizo daibutsu.

In this vein, there are four main gods of war: Hatchiman (patron of warriors); Marishiten (a goddess of light); Daikokuten (one of the seven gods of fortune); Bishamonten (one of the Four Heavenly Kings).

The Pentacle and the Grid

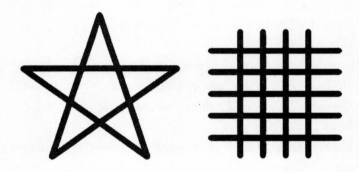

The *se-man* is the classic pentacle, a disc inscribed with a pentagram, a form of protection from evil or misfortune. The grid, *do-man*, is also used for protection and associated with the subject of *kuji* (see below). Both can be found embedded in magical literature in Japan and on objects such as armour and scrolls. Interestingly, the famous female free divers called *shima* who dive for shellfish and pearls in Mie prefecture wear headgear with one of these symbols on them to protect them on their long dives. The grid has a long history in Japan and is combined with the now very famous ritual called *kuji* – the art of the nine slashes.

The Art of *Kuji*

臨兵闘者皆陣列在前

No word resonates in the world of Japanese history and magic as strongly as the word *kuji*. The first thing anyone should understand about the series of mantras known as *kuji* is that it is has no clear definable boundaries and no clear origin, though it is most definitely not from Japan. It has multiple variations and distinct schools. The word *kuji* is a base word and concept that various methods of magic are founded upon. Furthermore, it should be known that some sources of *kuji* contradict each other and at points do not show symmetry. Some of the skills relevant to *kuji* were passed down in secret among specific groups, with their variations growing outwards as time progressed. It is only now, in this modern era, that we are bringing them back together as one – a realignment which has highlighted their differences.

The *kuji* used here are in the main (but not exclusively) taken from the following: *Otake Ritsuke*, the head teaching master of the Tenshin Katori Shinto Ryu, a fifteenth-century sword school; the academic work of the late Dr Carmen Blacker OBE of Cambridge University; an article by Dr Waterhouse; the samurai school Mubyoshi Ryu; and the collective work of the Japanese author Mr Y. Toyoshima.

The Four Main Areas of *Kuji*
Kuji, on a very basic and rudimentary level, can be broken into four parts, which may or may not have been known in full to the practitioners of old Japan.

Part 1: Kuji

The first area is the concept of *kuji* itself, which involves nine basic words of power:

Number	Japanese	Pronunciation
1	臨	Rin
2	兵	Pyo
3	闘	Toh
4	者	Sha
5	皆	Kai
6	陣	Jin
7	列	Retsu
8	在	Zai
9	前	Zen

These nine elements are accompanied by hand postures known as *mudra* and corresponding lines found on the *kuji* protection grid. They also are the platform for numerous *kuji* spells and should be considered the backbone of the practice and the basis of all its power.

Part 2: *Kuji In*

Perhaps the most famous element of the *kuji* magic system is the *kuji in*, or nine hand postures. A series of nine *mudra* hand postures that correspond to the nine power words given above are to be considered a set. Alongside the hand positions, a mantra is chanted for each *kuji*. According to Otake Ritsuke, the head teaching master of the Tenshin Katori Shinto Ryu sword school, the purpose of *kuji in* is to achieve a state of *muga* ('no-mind'), a state of extinguishment. By practising these hand postures and by chanting rhythmically, a person can train their mind to understand the essence of *muga* and thus call upon that state whenever they need to, perhaps in a time of difficulty or even in battle. Research suggests that *kuji* was originally a Taoist spell of protection, but, as will become clear, *kuji* is so varied that its meaning has changed over time.

Part 3: *Kuji Kiri*

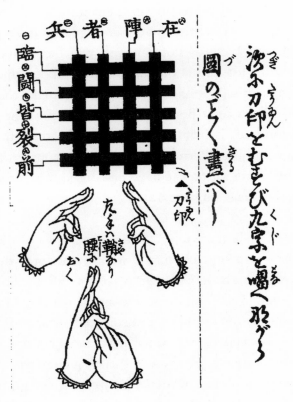

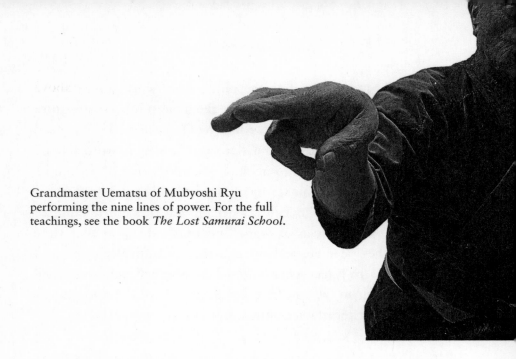

Grandmaster Uematsu of Mubyoshi Ryu
performing the nine lines of power. For the full
teachings, see the book *The Lost Samurai School*.

Kuji kiri is a form of protection grid cut into the air, written on
the palm of the hand, written on paper or placed upon objects as
a protection spell. It consists of nine lines which correspond to the
above *kuji* word list and is the basic matrix upon which the art
of *juji* ('tenth symbol') is based. A person will make the first line
or cut from left to right horizontally at the top of the grid, and
then the second cut is from top to bottom on the left. The grid
maker then continues alternating between horizontal and vertical
until all nine words of power have been used. The order can be
followed in the image on page 62.

Part 4: *Juji* – 'The Tenth Symbol'
Juji is a form of protective magic where you form the grid of
kuji kiri as shown above and then place a tenth symbol upon it.
This tenth symbol is a Japanese ideogram which always has a
meaning and thus fits in with the caster's intention. For example,
the dragon is associated with water in Japanese culture; therefore,
when crossing water a Japanese traveller would write the nine
lines of power and draw the ideogram for 'dragon' on top of the

grid, giving them the protection of the dragon and safety when crossing water. Other ideograms give other forms of protection.

The following list of *juji* is from the samurai school of Mubyoshi Ryu, a 400-year-old school which is now led by grandmaster Uematsu. The list shows which ideograms to use on top of the grid of power for different situations.

天   Use *Ten* (Heaven) before you meet high-ranking people
龍   Use *Ryū* (Dragon) when you across a sea, river or bridge
虎   Use *Ko* (Tiger) when you go through large field or deep mountain
王   Use *O* (King) when you go to battle or meet a thief
命   Use *Mei* (Life) when you eat without protection
勝   Use *Shō* (victory) when you quarrel or have a confrontation
鬼   Use *Ki* (demon) when you fight illness or go to an evil place
水   Use *Sui* (Water) when many people gather
大   Use *Dai* (large) when you are happy or something positive has happened
行   Use *Gyō* (to go) when you move to war or depart a place

Alternative *Juji* Spells

One variation of *juji* is taken from the *Nichiren* sect of Buddhism and is structured in a different way to the above. You must still use the above steps, but instead of drawing the *kuji* grid and placing the desired ideogram over it, this form of *juji* requires you to draw ten lines as shown in the image below. Start by drawing the line at the top left and move to the top right, then move back to the left and then right again until all ten are finished. This can be done in either the air or on paper. On each stroke call out the name of the ideogram as listed below. Notice how they differ from the standard *kuji* power words, and also remember that the tenth symbol is the last ideogram in the list. That means that the first nine are the words of power and the tenth word gives the spell direction.

To counter a curse and invoke disaster

1. Nen念
2. Pi波
3. Myo妙
4. Ho法
5. Riki力
6. To刀
7. Jin尋
8. Dan段
9. Dan段
10. E壊

To weaken the enemy and invoke disaster

1. Nen念
2. Pi波
3. Myo妙
4. Ho法
5. Riki力
6. Kan環
7. Jaku著

8. O於
9. Hon本
10. Nin人

To disperse the spirit of the dead or the living
1. Fu怖
2. I畏
3. Gun軍
4. Jin陣
5. Chu中
6. Shu衆
7. On怨
8. Shitsu悉
9. Tai退
10. San散

The Origins of *Kuji*

Kuji is said to have originated somewhere in the East, but in truth it is hard to know as it seems all researchers find themselves lost in the shadows of unknown history. One idea is that that it is a Taoist system, and it first appears in the Taoist *neipian* (inner chapters) of the *Baopuzi* by Ge Hong (283–343), which states that *kuji* is 'a prayer to avert evil influences and to ensure that things will proceed without difficulty'. The meaning behind the ideograms is also unknown, but according to David Waterhouse of Toronto University the ideograms form a grammatically perfect Chinese sentence:

臨兵闘者皆陣列在前
(*lin bing dou zhe jie chen lie zai qian*)

This he translates as, 'May those who preside over warriors be my vanguard.'

It is uncertain what the exact origins of this system are, but it is without doubt one of the oldest magic traditions recorded, already popular enough to be written about in the third century. All that can be said is that it came to Japan from mainland Asia and has been a widely practised form of magic in many traditions, spawning a myriad of variations.

The Basic Sword *Mudra*

Before you learn to draw the nine lines you have to understand what you will draw the lines with. To cut the lines in the air you will need to use the sword mudra. This is a symbolic sword represented by your middle and index fingers, with the ring and little fingers joined with the thumb.

In some traditions the 'sword' is housed in a 'scabbard', made by your opposite hand and placed at your hip before use, as though it were a real sword.

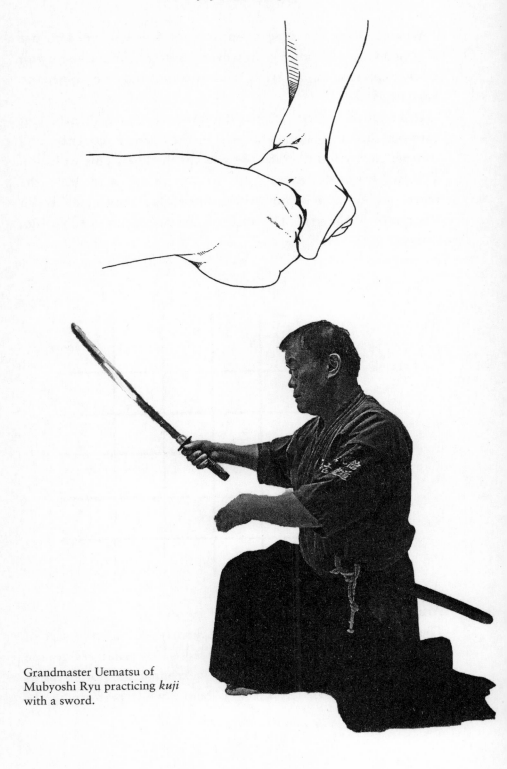

Grandmaster Uematsu of
Mubyoshi Ryu practicing *kuji*
with a sword.

When cutting the nine magical lines you will need to use the sword mudra above; however, as stated previously, *kuji* is an expansive and varied tradition and may be subject to variations.

Draw your sword or sword mudra from its sheath. Cut through the air, making the grid in the correct sequence, and call out each word of power as you cut the lines. This will form a protective spell around you. To move this on to *juji* – the tenth symbol, at the end write the corresponding ideogram in the centre of the grid. The spell can be finished by calling out, 'A-un!'

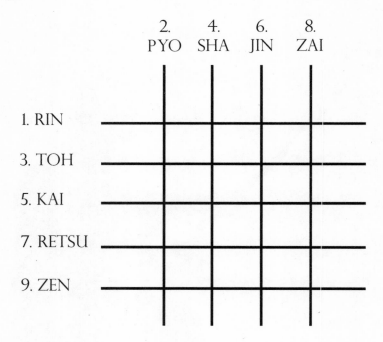

Alternative Forms of *Kuji Kiri*

The following *kuji kiri* spells are taken from *Nichiren* sect of Buddhism and should be considered as alternatives to the standard *kuji* described above. Simply exchange the power words above for the alternative versions below while performing the nine-line grid.

A *kuji* to attack the spirit of a dead person with a sword and to make it depart in peace

1. A阿
2. Noku耨
3. Ta多
4. Ra羅
5. San三
6. Myaku藐
7. San三
8. Bo菩
9. Dai提

A *kuji* to invoke disaster upon the spirit of someone who is still alive or to fight off an epidemic

1. Ryou 令
2. Hyaku 百
3. Yu 由
4. Jun 旬
5. Nai 内
6. Mu 無
7. Sho 諸
8. Sui 衰
9. Gen患

A *kuji* spell for all kinds of exorcisms

1. Ryou令
2. Hyaku百
3. Yu由
4. Jun旬
5. Nai内
6. Mu無
7. Sho諸
8. Sui衰
9. Gen患

A *kuji* spell to disperse or invoke disaster
1. Myo妙
2. Ho法
3. Ren蓮
4. Ge華
5. Kyo経
6. Ju呪
7. So咀
8. Doku毒
9. Yaku薬

A *kuji* spell for recovery from disease or to make an evil spirit depart in peace
1. Myo妙
2. Ho法
3. Ren蓮
4. Ge華
5. Kyo経
6. Doku毒
7. Byo病
8. Kai皆
9. Yu癒

To Expel Evil

In Indian mythology, the *Navagraha* are heavenly bodies which can bring about negativity but who are also worshipped, each with their own area of protection. To change this negativity or to rid yourself of evil influences, perform the following *kuji* ritual. This ritual is based on your age, chanting the *kuji* power words that are matched with your years.
1. Face south.
2. Chant the corresponding single *kuji* power word nine times (see below).
3. Clench the teeth nine times.

To understand which heavenly bodies are causing a negative effect and to discover which *kuji* to use for your age, utilise the following list. If you need to use an age higher than those within the lists, simply add nine to the last age provided for each *kuji*. Remember the Japanese traditionally start age from one, not zero, so you may need to subtract one from the ages in the list.

Kuji intoned	Heavenly body	Ages
Rin	Descending or South Node	7, 16, 25, 34, 43, 52, 61, 70
Pyo	The Sun	5, 14, 23, 32, 41, 50, 59, 68
To	Jupiter	9, 18, 27, 36, 45, 54, 63, 72
Sha	Mars	6, 15, 24, 33, 42, 51, 60, 69
Kai	Ascending or North Node	1, 10, 19, 28, 37, 46, 55, 64
Jin	Saturn	2, 11, 20, 29, 38, 47, 56, 65
Retsu	The Moon	8, 17, 26, 35, 44, 53 62, 71
Zai	Venus	4, 13, 22, 31, 40, 49, 58, 67
Zen	Mercury	3, 12, 21, 30, 39, 48, 57, 66

The following *kuji* spell was recorded by Carmen Blacker during her research into Japanese shamanism, but the use and context is not clear. Nonetheless, it serves as a great illustration of the diversity and intricacies of *kuji* magic and exemplifies how widespread and varied the art is.

1. Make all nine *kuji* hand symbols. As you make each one, call out its name: *Rin, Pyo, To, Sha, Kai, Jin, Retsu, Zai* and *Zen*. Make sure to call them out strongly and raise the voice to a sharp yell on the last *kuji*.
2. Make the sword mudra and cut the *kuji kiri* magic grid in the air.
3. Call out in Sanskrit, A-UN-A-UN ('the beginning and the end').

4. Call out the lesser spell of Fudo: '*No maku samanda basarada.*'
5. Repeat the heart sutra: '*Gyate gyate haragyate haragyate bochi sowaka.*'
6. Roar loudly and cry out, '*Shin*!'

Finally, it is also acceptable to chant the names of the *kuji* words of power while using a wooden sword and a rosary.

The above outline of *kuji* should give you a basic foundation in the use of the ritual spell, but keep in mind that there are a myriad of forms and traditions, that the hand *mudras* most likely have their origin in India, that the spell itself is probably Taoist and that in Japan it was used in many different situations. There are further examples of *kuji* in the remainder of this volume.

Wara Ningyo – Straw Curse Dolls

As far back as the sixth century the Japanese have had a form of doll used to curse their opponents; this was also recorded in the twelfth-century document *Heike Monogatari*, and by Hearn and others. The aim is to inflict misfortune and suffering – if not death – on the intended victim.

Instructions
1. Construct a doll made of straw.
2. Write the name and age of the victim on paper and insert it into the straw doll.
3. Draw the face of the enemy upon the doll.
4. At night, visit a shrine, temple or sacred space and find an old tree.
5. Place a *kanawa* or iron circlet upon your head which has three vertical spikes attached; these are used to secure three lit candles. (Hokusai, the Edo period artist, captured this circlet in his picture 'The hour of the Ox', shown opposite.

The hour of the Ox is a reference to the early hours between 1 a.m. and 3 a.m., and as you can see in the image, the woman is practising magic under the watchful gaze of the mythical *tengu* goblins.)

6. At the hour of the Ox, nail the straw doll to the ancient tree and your curse will chase your enemy.

Blowing Away 'Sin'

A doll which represents the human figure can also be used in rites of purification where the subject rubs the doll on their body or blows their breath upon it, thus transferring transgressions and pollutions they have to the doll, which is later cast into a river or another body of water. The doll can be made of material such as straw, wood iron or paper; the latter is the most common in modern Japan. The following extract was written in the mid-eighteenth century and instructs you on how to make a paper version of this doll:

How to make a magical paper doll

by

Ise Sadatake

1763

A *Nademono* (lit. thing to stroke) is a paper doll used when you ask an *Onmyo* magician to pray for you. The performer makes a paper doll and hands it to you, you then pass your hand over it and give it back to the performer. He prays over this doll. After praying he sometimes floats it down a river.

It is also called *Hinagata* or miniature figure. To make one, fold a piece of paper in two the with the fold at the top and cut out the shape as it is in the drawing. It can be of any size.

To make the head cut a diamond shape in one side and fold it up.

Make the cuts at the bottom as in the picture.

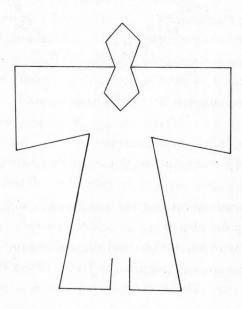

Divination by Turtle Shell or by the Shoulder Blade of a Deer

Ancient chronicles like the *Nihon Shoki* tell of divination through cracks in turtle shells or the shoulder blades of deer. To do this, take the shell or an animal shoulder bone and incise upon it the symbol *Machi*, as shown in the diagram below.

Ho / South

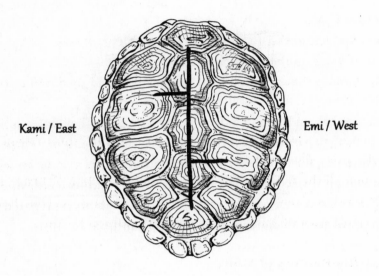

Kami / East   **Emi / West**

To / North

Take care here – notice that south is at the *top* of the diagram, which changes all of the directions – traditionally the Chinese used south for the top of their maps while Europeans used north. As you can see, south corresponds to the *tail* of the turtle shell, which is upright.

To acquire knowledge about the future, you have to ask a question that can be answered in a yes-or-no fashion. Then take the turtle shell or animal bone and cast it into a fire. When the first crack appears, you remove the shell and check the direction of the crack against the following list.

Positive Cracks
1. A crack in the north half and to the right
2. A straight crack in the north half
3. A crack in the south half and to the right
4. A straight crack in the south half
5. Cracks that go horizontal east or west
6. Cracks that go horizontal east or west and then point south

Negative Cracks
1. A crack in the north area and to the left
2. A crack in the south area and to the left
3. Cracks that go horizontal east or west and then point north

If you need to understand a dilemma and discover the ideal solution, you must prepare a certain amount of these shells or bones. In ancient times, for example, shells were burnt in this manner to select future virgin shrine maidens, one for each baby put forward; when a shell came up with a positive crack, that baby was then prepared for life to fulfil the role divination had set for her.

A Stick in the Road
To have a question answered, go to a road at dusk with a question in mind and plant a stick in the road. This is a representation the phallic god *Kunado*. Then listen to the talk of passers-by, and this will give you the answer to your question.

Stroking the Comb
As above, this magic spell is used to gain answers. Go to a crossroads with a comb of boxwood (*Buxus sempervirens*) and stroke it (most likely the teeth) across the sleeve of your kimono and speak or repeat the word '*tsuge*'. This means both 'box-wood' and 'inform me'. Then say the following three times: 'Oh god of cross-road divination, grant me a true response.' The answer will

come by the chatter of the next person to come past you, or even the third person. Sometimes an area around the practitioner would be cordoned off with rice to dispel evil. A similar version is given by Hadland-Davies, who calls it *tsuji-ura*. In this practice women listen to the conversations of passers-by and string together the prediction.

Ku Magic

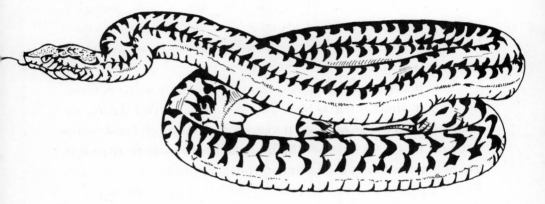

Ku magic is very evil and of Chinese decent. To practise this you are to collect as many venomous creatures as possible and place them all in a pot together. After a while of fighting and feasting only one creature will be left alive; this is now the *Ku* animal. This creature can bring you riches but it can also kill your enemy with ease. You can kill your enemy directly with it or you can let it run around their food, poisoning the meal, bringing death and disease.

This *Ku* creature is a powerful entity and is difficult to destroy. It is said that through it a magician will gain wealth and power and that any souls that the creature kills will serve the magician and not go on to the afterlife. Once it has been exposed to a feast it will contaminate the food with its evil, and when the guests eat they will die in fits of coughing blood, or the animals that the guests have eaten will be resurrected in their stomachs and kill them from the inside.

Some *Ku* creatures, like the golden caterpillar or the *Ch'in tsan*, are put in loaves of bread, wrapped up and left on the roadside; if a traveller picks it up and eats it, they will die and their soul will serve the magician.

Creating a Powerful Dog Talisman
The magic of *Inu Gami*: Tie up a hungry dog on a lead and place some food just out of reach. When the dog is at its hungriest and straining forward, cut off its head and place it in a vessel. This will make a powerful dog-deity to worship and use as the magician can command it to do their bidding.

The Vengeance of the Dog
Bury a dog in the ground up to its neck and cut off its head with a bamboo saw (a common execution technique in Japan). As it dies, say, 'If you have a soul, kill [insert name] and I will make you a god.' Then keep the dog's head and the dog will effect curses for you.

To Expel Crop Pests
Create a soldier made from straw and parade him around a field that is plagued by pests, then throw him into a river. This will expel the pests.

Calling up the Dead
Calling up the dead in Japan is sometimes as simple as reciting a poem or a passage addressed to the dead. This passage will call them to you and you may ask them to answer any questions that you have.

> Hear me, hear me,
> I call for today's water
> What water may I call for?
> I call for the water, the young spray
> Spirit, come with your sleeves bathed in tears

Spirit, come with your skirts full of dewdrops
We can only hear its voice and not see its form
We can hear the sound but not see the figure
It comes on seven or eight rapid currents
Come down to dance
It comes to give us an account

The spirit will come and you may ask questions of it.

A Spell to Deprive Someone of Their Senses
Below is a Shinto spell to deprive someone of their senses. It is said that Miyaji Suii learned this spell from a high-ranking eighteenth-century monk called Sugiyama Sosho. Simply chant this spell and clap your hands once at the end.

あんたりをん、そくめつそく、びらりやびらり、そくめつそく、ざんざんきめい、ざんきせい、ざんだりひをん、しかんしきじん、あたらうん、をんぜそ、ざんざんびらり、あうん、ぜつめい、そくぜつ、うん、ざんざんだり、ざんだりはん

(Antariwon, Sokumetsusoku Birariyabirari Sokumetsusoku Zanzankimei Zankisei Zandarihiwon Shikanshikijin Ataraun Wonzeso Zanzanbirari Aun Zetsumei Sokuzetsu Un Zanzandari Zandarihan)

The Art of *Toritsu Banashi* – Summoning the Dead
First you need a Shinto and Buddhist priest (not easy to find) to perform purification rituals of the area and put out incense and then make offerings of flowers and uncooked rice at the altar. The priest then takes a bow or bow-like tool and twangs it with his right hand, calling the name of the dead, then shouts 'kitazo yo!' over and over again. Kitazo means 'I have come', and the priest shouts this time and time again until his voice

changes and is replaced with the voice of the dead person being summoned. The dead person may then be asked questions, but it will answer briefly and will interrupt with calls of 'Hasten, hasten for my coming back is painful and I have little time to stay'. After the ghost has gone the priest will be unconscious. This ritual is said to have been performed in the strange story of Bikuni-san. This woman had lost her son and called him back from the dead, but when the son returned he told her not to mourn for it ailed him, instructing her instead to give offerings to the dead. She became a nun, childlike in nature, and loved all things that were miniature.

Shamanism

Shamanism has one foot in the prehistoric and one foot in the modern era. Almost dead in Japan, it can be classed as one of the oldest forms of magic in the world. However, it has no central or unified philosophy and varied according to time, location and lineage; it is therefore multifaceted and colourful but also hard to define. On the whole, shamans (for want of a better word) are predominantly female (shamanesses) but males are not unknown and therefore I will use the masculine term to mean both male and female. Of course a shaman in Japan would not call themselves a shaman, and they would not even understand the word, but the rites and rituals they perform fall under this broad term. The task of the shaman was to cure the sick, perform divination, mediumship and even telepathy, and also to go into trances.

You may be able to recognise a Japanese shaman walking along; they have a black bag on their back and a 'rosary' called an *Irataka no Juzu* consisting of 180 beads and badger fangs. They may have polished badger, fox or bear skulls, old coins, or all of the above and more. A shaman may make money on feast days or when travelling by communicating with the dead for relatives of those who have passed on. Also, when a local person dies, the village will put money together to call a shaman and have them perform the ritual of 'opening the mouth of the dead' to help the soul on its way.

Protecting Your Home from Evil

Remembering that the dead, demons, fox spirits and all kinds of strange creatures prowl the night in old Japan, it was essential to protect your home from invading monsters. The following are a few things that can be done to keep evil at bay and beyond the threshold.

The Family Shrine

From ancient times in Japan, Shinto, the way of the gods, has been a folk religion, and ancestor worship is a massive part of this. A Japanese family may maintain an *uji-gami* shrine where the dead members of the family collectively become 'the ancestors'. When someone passes over into the spirit world they can join the gods or collective souls who look after the family. Once dead, a person becomes a *hotoke-sama* in the Buddhist tradition and a *reijin* or *mikoto* in the Shinto tradition. Alternatively, there is the *hito-kami* (possibly *gami*), which is a holy place dedicated to a single personified spirit-god (*kami*). Both versions will protect and nurture the whole family and are a form of protection from evil or malice for the family – a fun way to understand this can be found in the Disney film *Mulan*, in which the titular character talks with her ancestors.

Keeping the Dead out of a House

To keep the dead out of a house in shamanistic traditions the following spell is used. This is also a spell to counter destructive spinning elements in nature such as tornados, and the twisted forces of the dead. There may be variations to this, depending on tradition; however, the basic elements are as follows:

1. Take female underwear and tear off a 'rag' section of it.
2. Twist it in a left direction (possibly tied in a knot or tied with string).
3. The twisted rag is rubbed between female legs to infuse it with female energy.
4. Scorch the charm at one end.
5. Stand with your back to a crossroads or facing the entrance to a house.

Then finish by saying the following spell:

Ghosts of the dead
Ghosts of animals
Make no entry into this house
But help yourself to these rags

Finally, place the rag near the doorway, the dead will then be barred entrance to the home.

In Japan you cannot walk into a house with shoes on; part of this tradition is down to the fact that it is bad to walk *out* of a house with shoes on. It is not certain why this is so but one theory is that samurai would prepare for war and armour themselves inside a house; they would walk out with their shoes on and go to battle – and perhaps death.

6

CASTLES, FORTIFICATIONS
AND ARCHITECTURE

Even the castle or house of a samurai was constructed in accordance with tradition and magic. While this involved a complex system, there are some rules that do govern the fundamentals and which are based on the Chinese system of Feng Shui. The ideal is as follows:

1. To the north there must be mountains
2. To the east there must be water
3. To the south it must be open land
4. To the west there must be a great road

As each of the directions is associated with a colour, the Japanese had a poem to help them remember this system:

A black tortoise to the north
A blue dragon to the east
A red sparrow to the south
A white tiger to the west

Kyoto, the old capital of Japan, is based on this principle, being situated according to the rules above.

The Demon's Gate
Sometimes the north-east is known as *Kimon* and is considered to be the realm of demons. In Tokyo today, the Kanda Myojin shrine

in Ochanomizu and the Kaneiji temple in Ueno are both north-east of the imperial palace, which was once Edo Castle, the home of the ruling Tokugawa family. This was deliberately arranged so that the two holy places would protect the castle from the demonic influences of that direction – a double north-east barrier, if you like.

It is not uncommon for the north-eastern corner of a building to have a cut-out like the image below to stop demons or to confuse them. Also, you can place a statue or image of a monkey on this corner to ward off evil.

The Rear Demon's Gate

The opposite direction, south-west, is called *Urakimon*, which translates to 'Rear Demons' Gate'. To add to the protection of Edo Castle outlined above, the Sanno Jinja shrine was built to the south-west; this was then backed up by Hikawa Jinja shrine and Zojoji temple, which both lie south-west of the castle.

Holly and Sardines

To keep demons out of your house you should take a sprig of holly and a roasted sardine head. Place the roasted sardine head on the end of one of the sprigs and tie it to the outside of

your house. It is said that the holly stabs the eye of the demon and the smell of the roasted sardine keeps them at bay.

Spell of Protection

To guard your house at night use the following spell for protection:

寝るぞ根太 頼むぞ垂木 梁柱 何事あらば起こせ屋根棟
(Listen to me floor joists, I'm going to bed, rafters, beams and pillars, you have control, roofs and ridges wake me up if needs arise!)

Bridges, Pillars and Platforms

Alongside houses and castles, bridges, pillars and platforms were also in need of protection. The following stories show how normally human sacrifice was needed to placat any angered spirits, deities and dragons.

The Legend of Matsuo Kotei and the Dragon Platform

Legend has it that when attempts were made to build a fake island platform near Kobe, the stone foundations kept washing away with the tide. A necromancer named Abe na Yasuuji said that they were trying to build on the site of a dragon's lair and that thirty people would need to be sacrificed and buried beneath the pillars of the platform. He proposed to use local travellers for this sacrifice, but there was an uproar at the very idea, so a young man named Matsuo Kotei gave himself up in sacrifice so that the dragon could be placated.

The Dragon of Enoshima

In the year 151 the island of Enoshima was plagued by a dragon, so a lady called Benten sent it to sleep with soothing music from her *koto* (a Japanese stringed instrument). The people then killed it while it slept, and a temple was erected on the site. One Hojo Tokimasa (1138–1215), from a famous samurai family, prayed here, and while he did so a goddess appeared to him with a dragon's tail coming from the rear of her kimono. She warned him that if he was unjust then the family would fall within seven generations – the family fell in 1333.

The Bridge at Nikko

Shodo Shonin was the founder of the first Buddhist temple in Nikko (now a national park). One day he saw clouds of four different colours in the distance. Trying to reach them, he came to a river which was raging before him; unable to cross, he prayed for help. On the opposite bank of the river a gigantic apparition appeared, robed in

blue and black and wearing a huge necklace of human skulls. The figure threw a green snake and a blue snake over the river so that they stretched from one bank to the other and a bridge was formed. After Shonin crossed the bridge of snakes, the figure disappeared.

The Pillar of Gensuke

Gensuke Bashira's story, like those above, involves sacrifice and architecture. It is thought to date from 1596–1614. The bridge over the Matsu River was being improved, but the masonry always collapsed. Therefore, the builders decided that the next person to cross the older bridge would be sacrificed to appease whatever was doing the mischief. That sacrifice was called Gensuke. He was killed and put beneath the pillar.

The Pillar of Ears (or Noses)

Mimidzuka is a monument at a temple in Kyoto which is said to have buried below it the severed ears of over 30,000 Koreans taken during the invasion of Korea in the sixteenth century. Other research shows that it was not ears but noses that were taken, which is probably correct. Noses used to be taken if heads were too numerous, and the norm in Japan was to take the top lip and the nose at the same time to show the stubble or moustache to prove that the nose was from a man. However, Hideyoshi, the lord in charge of Japan during the invasion of Korea, is said to have given this order (translated by Hawley):

Mow down everyone universally, without discriminating between young and old, men and women, clergy and the laity—high-ranking soldiers on the battlefield, that goes without saying, but also the hill folk, down to the poorest and meanest—and send the heads to Japan.

So, back came the noses and into the pile they went, a tribute to the slaughter of tens of thousands of Koreans – this is not a monument the Japanese promote, yet it still stands and remains a sensitive issue.

SELF-PROTECTION IN JAPANESE MAGIC

We often forget that the world of Japan was a dangerous place; even in the centuries of peace you still had to be careful of both humans and spirits. Therefore, one core element of the esoteric side of Japanese life was the idea of self-protection. This section does not really deal with human aggressors but more with the demonic.

The *Gunpo Jiyoshu* military manual (*c.* 1619) gives the following selection of spells to help protect a samurai in war or at home. For more sections of this manual see the book *Secret Traditions of the Shinobi*.

To Avoid a Fatality
To dispel fatality, you should chant '*On Ashirikakei Houkai*' seven times. Do this while facing the image of the god Nitten, and with your hands make the mudra *Naibaku In*:

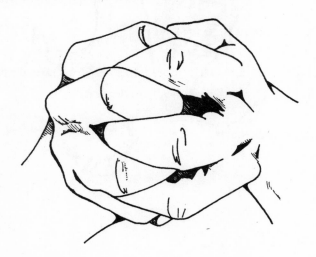

After that, make the mudra *Gejishi In* and chant the following three times:

Tensho Zeshin Koumyaku Shukunin Bosatsu Kekairai Ejo

Then make the mudra *Tensho In* and chant the above mantra three times again. Blow into your hands, put your palms together, and put them on your breast to keep the idea in your heart.

The Great Secret of Marishiten, the Goddess of War

Before you go to battle, chant the following three times:

Me-i-go-san-kai-jo-u, Go-go-jippo-ku-u, Hon-rai-mu-to-za-I,
Ka-sho-u-nan-boku

Then chant this poem three times:

In a storm, the wind from the mountain shall blow away and clear
all the enemies I am defying.

Lastly, chant three times:

On Marishiei-sowaka.

The above is a prayer for success in war; it is used from the general down to the lower-ranking samurai (*hamusha*).

The *Gunpo Jiyoshu* continues again with a spell for waking you up in an emergency; similar spells appear in other schools and are normally used to wake you if there is an intruder in your home or fortification.

The Secrets of Pillows
Version One

When you go to sleep, trace the ideogram 大 (large) three times on your left palm and then lick it. Details to be orally transmitted.

Version Two

Trace the Sanskrit letters above on to your pillow with the letter toward you and sleep on it. Then chant the following poem three times:

うちとけて　もしもまどろむ　ことあらば　引きおどろかせ　我
がまくら神

(If I am unguarded and fall into a doze, may my Pillow Gods startle
me so that I awaken)

A Secret Method to Bind Somebody to Secrecy

To bind somebody to secrecy, make the mudra of *Gejishi*
(shown below) and with it on your lips chant the following
poem three times:

秋津嶋　みもすそ　川のながれにて　わがためあしき　人は口なし

(Akitsushima in the flow of the River Mimosuso, may people
hostile to me have no mouth)

The above is to win when you argue in court; a lord should
chant this without fail after he has had a secret conference.

The *Zoho Majinai Chohoki Daisen* manual has a method to keep a person silent:

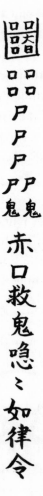

Protection from Injury

This is a secret method to pray so that a samurai can obtain victory without being injured on a battlefield. First make a mudra of *Gejishi* (see image left) and chant the following:

Shi-shi Fu-shu-se-tsu Ga Ho-u-myo-u Nanshi Shozo-cho-man-sha-mon-hitu fu-kyoshin

If you do this you will not be injured or hit by an arrow. Whether it is the lord himself or a soldier of low rank, if you think you are going to fight the enemy, chant this spell. This is a deep secret. This secret method was given to Zhang Liang by Huang Shigong.

The Secret Method of Yoshitsune

When you pass a very dangerous place, write these five characters on paper and put it into your topknot.

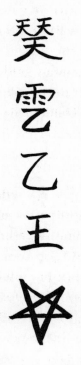

Then chant the following seven times:

On Kiru-kiru Mata-uji-yakuyasei-sowaka

Next, perform *kuji* seven times (Rin, Pyo To, Sha, Kai, Jin, Retsu, Zai, Zen). By doing this, you can protect yourself against arrows and swords even if passing before the enemy. Even at normal times, do this when you need to travel through a mountain pass at night or travel a long distance. It is said that this is the way Yoshitsune and was taught by Taro-bo, who was a *Tengu* goblin of the mountain Atago.

A Secret Method to Stop a Ninja or Thief

To stop an assailant, make a brush of Muku wood (*Aphananthe aspera*) on the day of *Kanoe* when it also corresponds with the Day of the Monkey, and write the following spell on all four sides inside the gate (lintel, two sides and threshold):

南無五大力菩薩　南無光明天王ソハカ　天ヨ天ヨ天ヨ鳳吉留留凧噫噫如律令

Also when you search for *shinobi* (ninja) or a suspicious person, first write the spell as above and put it on each exit, so that the person will not be able to exit. It is said this talisman was passed down by Nichiren Shonin to the Hakone Gongen shrine.

The Art of Preventing Robbers or Scoundrels

On the seventh day of the seventh lunar month in the hours of Snake (9–11 a.m.) or Horse (11 a.m.–1 p.m.), pick up a leaf of the Nurude tree (*Rhas javanica var. Roxburghii*) and write the *kuji* (grid) upon it. On the thirteenth day of the lunar month, grind it into powder and mix glue with it and make pills. Scatter them in the direction from which you think the enemy will approach; this will prevent robbers from coming and will protect you from an epidemic too. The number of leaves with *kuji* grids written on them (to be ground into powder) should be 360 while you chant the *kuji* power words a myriad of times.

Becoming Invisible to the Enemy

Take the placenta of a woman's first baby without letting her know and then dry it in the shade for 100 days while you chant the nine *kuji* over it 1,000 times every day.

Also, take the fangs from a live *mamushi* pit viper, and put them into your topknot in case of an emergency. If a scout or captain of a shinobi night attack carries this, the squad will not be seen by the eyes of the enemy. However, if they have doubts or use this skill for their own evil desires, they will meet their nemesis and will be discovered by the enemy.

Bringing a Robber Back to Justice

A person who has woken to find their house robbed could do the following to bring the thief back:

1. Find the footprints of the burglar
2. Burn a good quantity of Moxa in each print within the garden

As the Moxa burns, the robber will feel as if their feet are on fire and will gain no rest until they return with the goods or for justice.

The *Zoho Majinai Chohoki Daisen* manual also has spells that help catch thieves; this manuscript is kept in the John Rylands Library, Special Collections Section, a division of Manchester University Library.

Zoho Majinai Chohoki Daisen Spell 1
Write the spell below and stand in the footprints of a thief to discover who the thief is or where your stolen property is.

Zoho Majinai Chohoki Daisen Spell 2
An alternative to the previous spell.

Zoho Majinai Chohoki Daisen Spell 3

After writing this in the air and toward the front and back of the house, you may go to sleep. This way the thief will leave without stealing anything – or if he comes into the house during your absence, he will be unable to move from there.

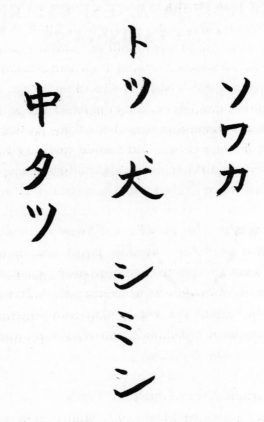

8

ANCIENT JAPANESE CHARMS AND TALISMANS

This chapter will describe various kinds of magic charms and talismans from a variety of periods and geographical locations across Japan. Here you will encounter spells and rituals that concentrate on the darker side of magic – lighter ones do exist in the lore, but we are concerned with the more hellish among them.

Protecting a Child Who Has Passed Away

Jizo is the saint of children, and in Japan a woman can buy a stamp of the saint and stamp the image of the saint 100 times on small sections of white paper. On the fortieth day after the burial of the child, the woman kneels down by a running stream or river and drops each paper individually in to the water and chants the prayer, '*Namu JizoDai Bosatsu.*'

Getting Rid of an Angry Ghost

One shamanic case in Japan tells of how a woman is haunted by her dead husband's spirit and how he is angry at her and wishes her to honour him after death by not marrying again. To counter the angry ghost, the shaman follows this magic ritual:

1. Repeat the heart sutra 100 times: *Gyate gyate haragyate haragyate bochi sowaka.*
2. Promise the dead spirit his wishes will be fulfilled.
3. Shout out the nine *kuji* words of power.

With this the angry ghost disappeared, and the illness the woman had been suffering vanished with it.

All of the following talismans should be kept in a small cloth bag unless the instructions say otherwise.

To Dispel Nightmares
When you have had a nightmare, trace this charm on your palm.

To Travel Safely at Night

If you carry this charm in your kimono, you will not come in harm's way.

A Talisman for Travelling in the Dark of Night
Carry this with you when travelling on a dark night and it will
bring you luck.

喼

急

如

律

令

To Destroy a Hated Enemy

Write down your enemy's name on some deutzia wood (*Deutzia crenata*) and bury this talisman with their name on it. In this way you can take vengeance upon them.

To Expel Evil or the Spirits of the Dead

If someone who is plagued by the spirits of the dead uses this, it will expel the spirits.

Protection from Curses

If you carry this talisman, you will not be cursed.

To Take Revenge on Those Who Have Cursed You
Use this talisman to reverse the effects of a curse put upon you.

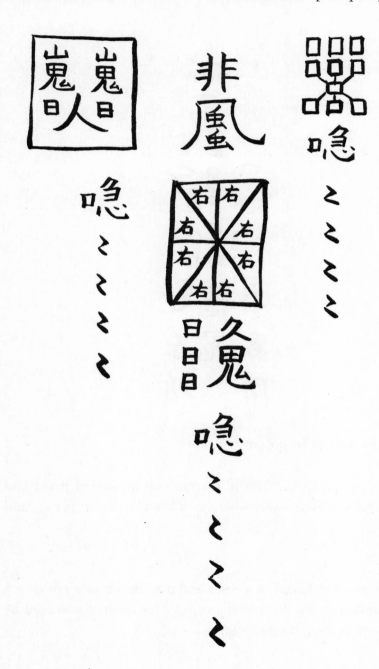

To Protect Against Robbery
Use this talisman in your home to protect your property from thieves.

To Make a Man Impotent
Version 1
Wipe the sperm of the man in question on a piece of paper and hide it under a Tatami mat where people will often cross over and step on it.

Version 2
Carve a wooden model of a penis and dry roast it in a pot over a flame while moving the model around. This method was used by prostitutes up until the early 1900s.

A Spoken Charm to Deter the Attention of an Unwanted Man

我念ふ君の心ははなれつる我も思はじ君も思はじ

(Your affection for me will move away so that I will not love you and you will not love me either)

The Power of Demon Charms

There is a form of talisman that relies on the power of the Japanese *oni* or demon. Each of the following talismans has a standard ideogram at the top which represents the word for demon as seen above. It is then given direction by adding a specific command.

鬼

The above is the ideogram for 'demon' and is used in all the following charms (the charm is at the top and its use is at the bottom of each image).

To Attract a Woman

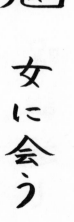

To Fulfil a Wish

魁叶

願
望
諸
事

To Return a Curse

魃鈑

呪
詛
返
し

To Recover from Disease

病気平癒

For a Long Life

延命祈念

For a Woman's Love

魁男

女に思われる

For Safe Travel upon Water

鬼一

水上安全

A Talisman for Luck

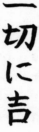

一切に吉

9

SAMURAI AND THEIR WEAPONS OF DEATH

The samurai had a certain amount of superstition and religion surrounding their weaponry, and they also called on the divine to aid them in their battles. This section will allow you a brief glimpse into the world of the warrior and how there is a darker tradition behind their weapons and armour.

Arrows and Quivers

The samurai quiver was modelled in abstract on the head of an unknown demon called Isoso. Legend says that the god Taishakuten killed this demon with twenty-five arrows, which led to the tradition of the samurai carrying twenty-five arrows at a time. Further to this, they would single out one arrow which would be used to fire in an unlucky direction to 'kill' negativity. Also, some traditions say that the samurai must keep at least one arrow on him for when he is dead.

If you want to kill a snake or demon, drip human saliva on the arrowhead as this is deadly to demons, snakes, dragons and giant centipedes. (Keep in mind that in some places in Japan it is bad to kill a snake; if you do, its severed head will appear by magic in your rice box.)

The Bow

Archery was used during official inspections of decapitated heads. A lord would have archers standing by him, ready to aim and shoot at the ghost that belonged to the decapitated head, defending the lord against the vengeance of the dead samurai.

When making a bowstring for a samurai bow, it is said women were not allowed near the string or to touch it, as they were formed from *yin* energy and would have negative effects on the weapon. In addition to this, it was a definite taboo for a woman who was menstruating to touch anything that was involved in the making of a bow.

The *Gunpo Jiyoshu* manual instructs the following for when a samurai lord rides to war:

> Hold the bow with left hand and twang the string with the right hand, concentrating your mind on the gods and driving away evil spirits or ghosts. This is called *meigen* or 'sounding the string'. After doing this, pray for the children, the domain and then the clan, then unstring the bow while uttering the name of the god '*Hachiman Daibosatsu*' – but say this only once.

Raiko is a legendary figure in Japanese folklore, and a mean archer. It is said that he went on a quest to kill all the demons and goblins in Japan. One night, a woman came to him in his dreams and gave him a magnificent bow and taught him the deepest secrets of archery to help him on his quest. He came to a place littered with human remains where devils drank human blood – their 'merriment' was cut short as the famed archer killed them all.

Also, one archer is said to have twanged his bow three times to expel a demon that was causing his father to be ill.

The Sword

Katana-kagi is a form of prayer with a sword, used to cut down evil demons and expel them from a person who is ill. You should take up a sword and beckon and cut the demon with the blade, doing so above the head of the ill patient. This cutting action was believed to destroy the demon's hold on the ill person, and they were said to recover after this.

Bloodthirsty Swords

Legend tells that the swords made by the swordsmith Muramasa Sengo or his school were demonic blades that possessed the madness of their creator and thirsted for human blood. However, interestingly, it is possible that this tale was initiated by the famous shogun Tokugawa Ieyasu. It is said his father and grandfather were killed by swords from Sengo's foundry, and others from the same workshop were also used by samurai who rebelled against both of the above deceased men. Therefore, Tokugawa Ieyasu forbade his retainers from wearing swords of that line and it is possible that the legend of their demonic power was established to make good the name of his ancestors and to show that they were not incompetent rulers.

Three Heads in a Cauldron

Once there was a warlord who had two ingots of iron. He sent them to a smith to have a sword forged from them. However, the smith made two swords at the same time, a bonded pair. One was female and one was male. One he gave to the king as requested, and the other he gave it to his wife to bury; he instructed her that if anything should happen to him, when their son came of age she should give him the sword. Time passed, and the king noticed that his sword was constantly wet, covered by dew. His ministers said that this was because the sword had a matching partner – because they were separated, the sword was crying in lamentation. The king immediately knew what had happened and sent for the smith. The smith was then tortured and killed, but he did not give away the position of the other sword. The wife and son fled, taking the sword with them. Later, one of the king's ministers, Hakuchu, became disgruntled and hated the king, so he sought out the smith's son to help him attain vengeance. He found the son and the wife and explained all. The son, seeing it as a sign from the gods, bit off the end of the sword; keeping it in his mouth, he had Hakuchu cut off his head. Hakuchu took the head to the king, but the king looked at the face and thought it evil, so had the head boiled for twenty-one days. However, after that period the head had not changed at all. Hakuchu told the king that the head wished to speak to him and so the king looked into the cauldron, bending over and getting up close. The head of the smith's son spat out the sword point, decapitating the king, whose head now fell into the water of the cauldron. The two heads began to fight and bite each other. Hakuchu, watching all this, thought that the king's head was getting the upper hand and so put his head over the cauldron and cut his own head off, attacking the king's head alongside that of the smith's son. Thus there were three heads in a cauldron, and all over a missing sword.

This theme can also be found in a story in which a samurai called Yoshihiro goes to kill a political prisoner, Morinaga. In a weakened state, Morinaga bit off the end of Yoshihiro's sword so that he might have posthumous vengeance like the smith's son, but when Yoshihiro took his head and killed him he noticed the sword point and threw the head away, taking heed of the story of the Three Heads in a Cauldron.

The Arrow Cape

One less famous section of the samurai arsenal was the *Horo* or arrow-catching cape. This consisted of layers of material tied to the samurai that was used in two ways:

1. To be tied to the rear and allowed to balloon as the samurai galloped back to his line of battle, the purpose of which was to stop arrows from penetrating the rear of his armour.
2. To hold over the front and above the head with the arms extended, to catch arrows.

This arrow cape in samurai lore represented the placenta in the womb and was considered 'safe', as though a warrior was inside of his mother.

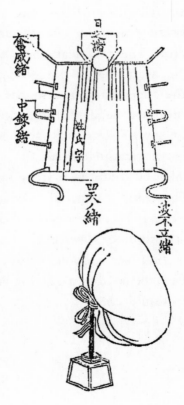

The Fan

A samurai fan should have ten 'ribs' which represents the great virtues in Buddhism:

1. Refrain from killing living things.
2. Refrain from stealing.
3. Refrain from sex.
4. Refrain from lying.
5. Refrain from taking intoxicants.
6. Refrain from taking food at inappropriate times.
7. Refrain from singing, dancing, playing music or attending performances.
8. Refrain from wearing perfume, cosmetics and decorative accessories.
9. Refrain from sitting on high chairs and sleeping on luxurious, soft beds.
10. Refrain from accepting money.

The *Book of Samurai* tells us that samurai accepted gold by having the coins placed on the front of a fan, while decapitated heads to be presented were placed on the rear face of the fan. For this reason some fans were painted with a mottled snow effect so show the pattern of blood drops which would remain after the head was disposed of.

Armour
The Costume of Death
If a samurai wished to announce his intention to be victorious on the field of battle or die without retreating, he would create the costume of death. This was done by cutting short the ties fastening his helmet and armour to indicate that he would not be tying them again, meaning that he was riding to his death and would not be returning or that he would only return if victorious. Furthermore, if a samurai was set on killing a superior because of a grudge, he would wear this consume of death before he made the kill – thus anyone found in such a get-up would be questioned as to his intentions.

The Hole in the Helmet
At the top of a samurai helmet is a small ventilation hole; tradition says that the 98,000 gods of war enter into the samurai through this hole to give him power.

Sweet-smelling Helmets
Samurai may burn incense inside of their helmet so that when they are killed their head will smell sweet to the enemy.

Ghost Bodyguards
Legend holds that in the tenth-century war known as Tenkei no Ran, one of the major players, Masakado, had an arch-enemy called Tawara Toda (sometimes Hidesato). To protect himself, Masakado employed phantom doppelganger bodyguards that looked and talked just like he did. Toda, wanting to find the real Masakado, moved through the crowds, feeling for a pulse on each figure until he found the one with a pulse, at which point he cut him down. It has actually been postulated by some that the story is based on real events. Masakado apparently feared the awesome archery skills of Toda, so he had five of his retainers dress just like him on the battlefield and move around, hoping to draw off his enemy's fire. Toda killed three before he finally identified the real Masakado and brought him down.

The Samurai Ancestral Home

Haunted manor houses, castles with bloody histories and spectres in the gardens are all seen by the English-speaking world as a Western idea, chilling us at Christmas as we revisit old legends (people have actually forgotten that ghost stories are a Christmas tradition; remember Dickens's *A Christmas Carol*). However, Japanese folklore has its fair share of family hauntings attached to the ancient warrior families and their castles. According to the *Budoshoshinshu* (paraphrased here from William Scott Wilson's translation), each and every ancient family home, be it castle, fortified manor house or simple residence, has its blood-filled history and its own ghosts.

Usually it involves the ghost of a low-ranking samurai who, wishing for vengeance due to mistreatment, attacks or infects a samurai who has the virtues of a true knight and therefore dies from a wound or from illness. The example given in the text is of Takeda Shingen and his retainer Amari Saemon, who people believed was killed by the clan's ghost.

The second way a ghost manifests itself is by taking possession of a samurai retainer who gives bad advice and brings the clan to ruin, becoming similar to Wormtongue from Tolkien's world. The manual states that there are six ways that this malignant spirit can use its host to cause problems:

1. He has power to stop a lord hearing good council.
2. By replacing honourable advisors with men of a mean ilk who are under the ghosts sway.
3. The possessed retainer will inform the lord that having children is paramount and brings suitor-wives below his station, alongside this promoting dancing, games and women until the lord is far from the path of righteousness.
4. With all the ostentatious entertainment, the clan treasury is empty; at this point the ghost will use its host to get the lord to fill its coffers by taxing the people, bringing locals

to hate their lord and to be poor and in the end causing all forms of monetary issues.

5. The ghost will then disapprove of military training and the upkeep of the clan's equipment and military prowess, bringing all the retainers to a state of uselessness.

6. All of the above lead to the ruin of the lord; this is the way a devil will enter a retainer and destroy a clan (or is an excuse for bad management).

Samurai Training

Maybe the greatest weapon for a samurai is the training endured to become a warrior of great achievement. In an example of samurai training, Hearn tells us that samurai boys were taken to execution grounds to witness gruesome executions and were to do so without a show of emotion; this exercise was adopted to vanquish any internal horror. He goes on to state that when returning home, the samurai boys were given blood-coloured rice to make sure fear was eradicated from their minds. To further stamp out any fear, they were told to go to the execution grounds at night and take the heads of the dead to show they had no terror left in them.

Seppuku – Ritual Suicide

The Japanese ritual of *seppuku* (self-disembowelment) is identifiable to most people and comes with two major names: 切腹 (*seppuku*) *and* 腹切 (*hara-kiri*).

The most popular word for Japanese ritual suicide is *hari-kari*, but this is a mispronunciation of the correct term, *hara-kiri*. The two names above are actually two uses of the same ideogram but reversed. *Seppuku* is 切 (cut) and 腹 (belly), while *harakiri* is 腹 (belly) and 切 (cut). The former is more formal while the latter is more casual.

Seppuku Facts

It can be voluntary or enforced. A warrior may take their own life if the battle is lost.

To be decapitated when bound is disgraceful but to be decapitated after cutting one's own belly is a high honour.

If a warrior refused to commit suicide it could ruin the entire family.

Originally there was no second or assistant, but as time progressed the position of *kaishakunin* was introduced; this was a friend who decapitated the victim to make his passing quicker as death by disembowelment was excruciatingly painful and could last hours.

The handle of the dirk used to commit suicide was taken off and the blade wrapped in paper so that the prospective suicide could not use it to fight his way out of the situation.

The inspecting officer would sit approximately three metres away so that the prospective suicide could not grab his sword and fight his way out.

The *kaishakunin* would stab the victim through the heart from behind if they thought that they were going to move to attack.

The goal of the assistant was to leave the skin of the throat attached so that the head did not roll around after decapitation – a difficult cut.

The assistant had their own assistant who would take over if they found it difficult to perform the deed.

Samurai women may perform *seppuku* by inserting a dagger into their throat.

The victim may secure their legs so that when they die they fall correctly.

One of the last *seppuku* rituals to take place was that of actor and writer Yukio Mishima, who in 1970 seized a military official to further his political aims. Failing in his attempted coup, he then committed ritual suicide. It is thought that the event was brought about to provide a stage for him to perform the ritual.

Different Types of Execution

Sensu-bara

A substitute for *seppuku* where the victim takes up a fan instead of a dagger; when they take up the fan they are decapitated.

Mizu-bara

This substitute for *seppuku* appears as two versions. The first is recorded by Seward, who says that a cup of water is lifted up instead of a dagger, at which point the decapitation occurs. The second states that the person to be beheaded will dip their finger into water and use the moist finger to make a symbolic cut on the abdomen, at which point they are beheaded.

Te-bara

Another substitute for *seppuku* where an imaginary cut with the hand is made and the victim is decapitated.

Uchi-kubi

A criminal kneels down and hangs their head, at which point they are decapitated.

Shibari-kubi

A criminal is bound with their hands behind their back as they kneel down. An assistant will lift their toes off the ground from behind so that they lean forward, at which point they are beheaded.

Hiyaburi

To be burnt alive at the stake. This punishment was largely doled out to arsonists, but there are also examples of Christians being killed this way.

Nokogiribiki

A person is restrained and their head is sawn off.

Haritsuke

Crucifixion. The only difference to the Western style is that the legs are splayed and spears are jabbed into the torso in an X-shape.

Seppuku and punishment is an extremely interesting topic; for a full understanding see *Seppuku* by Rankin and *Hara-kiri* by Seward.

Skinning a Human Face

As discussed previously, if there were too many decapitated heads to bring back from a victory, a samurai leader may give the instruction for noses to be taken instead. However, it is not only noses that should be cut; in fact it is quite wrong to take *only* the nose, because some samurai may not be as honourable as their reputation and in the face of disgrace they may actually kill women or monks to secure a nose and claim a kill. To combat this, the rule of skinning the face came into play. The samurai would have to cut from around the top lip and base of the nose, around and up to the eyebrows, or they would have to cut down from the top lip and around the chin. Using either of these methods would prove that it came from a warrior male, as warriors tended to have facial hair and women would change their eyebrow shape. In addition to this, it was recommended that the samurai bring back the sword or a part of the helmet from the fallen foe. All of these were measures to stop a samurai cheating his way to a quick reward.

10

DEALING WITH THE DEAD

The way of life for a samurai was that of killing. His job was warfare and business was good, especially in the Sengoku period, which is also known as the Warring States period.

The following is a sermon for the dead, and if this spell is chanted the fallen dead will immediately attain Buddhahood and enlightenment; this is done so that a samurai will not be cursed or given over to divine punishment for killing their enemy.

諸悪本末無明来実検直儀何処有南北
(Shoaku honnmatsu mymyourai jikken chokugi kashoyu nanboku)

Incense is also used in connection with the dead and comes from Buddhist traditions. Putting incense near a body protects the departing soul from dealing with malevolent spirits. However, this does not seem to deter *jiki-ko-ki*, who are 'incense goblins' who love to devour smoke. Also, there is the belief that if you light incense and concentrate on someone who is dead then you can cause their soul to manifest itself in the smoke. One example is the old Chinese legend of Emperor Wu of the Han dynasty, who called to have spirit-summoning incense brought to him so he could see his dead love, the Lady Li.

Receiving Decapitated Heads

Inspecting a decapitated head was a very magical and supernatural experience. The enemy may be physically dead, but it was still considered to be dangerous as the spirit of the dead enemy was thought to be vengeful at this point. Therefore, some rules were set in place to ensure the safety of the lord and his home from the retribution of the fallen warriors:

> Sometimes the head was not allowed inside some parts of the camp or residence and should be shown at the gate.
> The lord was to be dressed for battle and armoured.
> Archers should stand on either side of the lord to protect him from the ghosts of the enemy.
> The lord should never look directly at the head; he should glance to it from his left side and maybe over a fan or sleeve.
> There should be someone who is born in the year of the horse present at the ceremony.
> A war cry should be given and dedicated to the gods of war.

When samurai used to categorise the decapitated heads of their victims they would put them into five basic groups: right-eyed, left-eyed, heaven-eyed, earth-eyed, buda-eyed (half closed).

However, it is said that there is one more type of head – a head that should not be shown to the lord, the 'head of hatred'. This is a head which is distorted and set grimaced, left-eyed and with a clenching of the teeth. These unsightly heads should not be shown to a lord.

Preparing Decapitated Heads

To wash decapitated heads you should start with the lower ranks. If the head belonged to a man of position, comb the hair and tie it with a twisted string made of paper. If it is the head of lower-ranking samurai or soldier, just tie it with left-handed rope.

The Headboard

The board for a head to rest on should be 24 cm square. It should have an upward-facing nail to fix the head in place and the corners should be rounded off. The whole thing should be made of Chinaberry wood.

The Box for the Head

The box in which a samurai would place a head should be 45 cm high, 24 cm in diameter and should bear a swastika written on the cover. Sew two pieces of fabric together and wrap the container with the cloth and secure it at the top with a knot. When the container is sent with the head back to the family, put a *kibo* arrow across and under the knot of the cloth covering the box to make the head presentable.

Poking the Eyes of the Dead

To help get a head ready for presentation, the samurai would sometimes use the pommel of his sword to push the dead eyes deeper into their sockets. They would also use a long, thick pin which rests alongside their sword in the scabbard to push the tongue back in the mouth. Also they would pull out the eyelashes to help keep the eyes closed and sometimes the teeth were blackened with an iron solution as a sign that the head had a high place of honour (as only lower people had unstained white teeth).

The Book of Heads

On a Japanese battlefield after a day of conflict, each samurai would bring his prized head with a piece of evidence to show that he had killed a real warrior. If the head was accepted, the deed would then be written in the book of heads so that he could be rewarded correctly at a later date.

Disposing of Heads

See image on page 48. The enemy heads should be thrown away in the direction of *Shikan* 死喚. To find out this magical direction, count the appropriate spaces on the diagram provided there.

On the days of the Rat, the Horse, the Hare and the Cockerel, count clockwise nine directions when counting from the Hare (you should start counting from one on the day mentioned; therefore, an example of the direction of *Shikan* is the direction of the Monkey if counting from the Rat – nine places including the start point).

On the days of the Ox, the Ram, the Dragon and the Dog, *Shikan* is the ninth direction counting from the Dragon.

On the days of the Tiger, the Monkey, the Snake and the Boar, *Shikan* is the ninth direction counting from the Snake.

After finding the correct direction, take the heads and gibbet them; this will make the ghosts of the heads call their fellows and lure them to their death, for the dead always want company.

The heads of aristocrats and generals should be gibbeted on chestnut wood while lower-ranking heads should be put on pear tree wood. When a number of heads are to be gibbeted, put up a chestnut wooden post on the right and a pear wooden post on the left, then put silk tree wood across them. The head of the general or lord should be wrapped in a *horo* arrow-cape when gibbeted; this is called *Buddha-gake*.

A Ritual over the Dead

In the morning, stand east of your encamped position and face westwards. Stab a *togariya* (reinforced arrow) into the ground beside the head of the dead person, hold a short samurai

horsewhip while making the *Naibaku* mudra and chant the
following words:

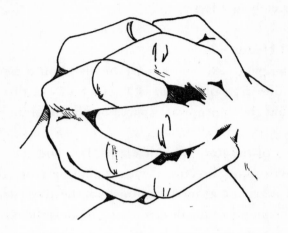

能く死する者は能く死して治す。円相を廻らして念仏す。
(*Those who die well will die to be at peace, I pray to Amitabha for
the creation of Enso, that is, the highest form of enlightenment*)

After that, hold the rod in your right hand and take the cord of
the whip in the left hand and put it across your breast. Then, with
the dead person on the floor, move backwards seven steps and
chant the *Komyo shingon* mantra seven times:

*On a-bokya be-i-ro-shano-u makabo-dara mani handoma jinbara
harabaritaya un*

This is then followed by the next mantra ten times:

Na-mu-amida-butsu

Next chant the words of Meigo (words of delusion and
enlightenment – unknown at this point) and wipe the whip three
times with paper. Turn left so that you turn your back to the dead

person and throw this rod away without taking it in your hand again. This is a way passed down from Zhang Liang.

To send the spirit of a decapitated warrior safely to the afterlife, recite the following words to the soul of the person:

看々きう業南無藕礙なるかな、心をひるがへし又生死を離れしめ
よ

(*Behold what you have done in your previous life and how it is. You should change your mental state so that you will leave the matter of life or death behind*)

By doing this, no matter how malicious the head is, it will not harm you nor take its revenge.

Death in Modern Japan

In Japan, Buddhism controls death – funerals are mainly Buddhist and they are not cheap. It costs to keep a gravesite in a cemetery and rituals need to be performed a few times after the main funeral, making Buddhist funeral direction a very lucrative business to be in.

When Japanese people die, they often do not use their names on their gravestones; instead they will posthumously be given a 'death-name'.

Food offerings left for the dead may be given to house elders or to pilgrims, but if children steal the food they will be cursed with a bad memory and stupidity.

In some parts of Japan they search the bones of a cremation and look for a bone from the throat area; if it has a Buddha image on it, the person will be enlightened in the next life.

To this day the dense forest of Aokigahara is a very popular destination for suicide, with 105 bodies found in 2003 alone. It is believed that the area was used for the practice of *ubasute* up to the nineteenth century; this is the practice of leaving elderly family members to die in a remote place. Their ghosts are said to haunt the place today.

11

ILL OMENS AND THE CHI OF DEATH

A bad omen can be something mundane and normal. They came in many guises, and the Japanese even had specialists called *gunbaisha* (esoteric tactician) who were trained in seeing the *chi* of the sky and what the heavens had in store for an army. For instance, if a kite or crow comes towards you when you depart for battle, it is considered a greater bad sign. However, all will be well if it flies away immediately after you have shot at it with a *Hikime* (whistling arrow).

Seeing *Chi* in the Sky

Chi, or the concept of seeing *chi* in the sky, is a large part of Japanese culture. Generals would have *gunbaisha* observe the enemy, their positions, villages, castles and so on. Depending on the colour and the shape of their *chi*, these seers could predict what was to happen in any given building or describe what the situation was like inside. The following is a reduced collection of images with descriptions which have been taken from the *Gunpo Jiyoshu* military manual (*c.* 1619) and which concentrate on the darker outcomes to be found by observing *chi* in the sky. For the times listed in the text see the diagram on page 48.

The *Chi* of the Death Fire

As seen in the picture above, if the smoke is surrounding the house and is not rising up to the sky, it is greater bad luck and the lord may be killed in battle. Therefore, it is called the Death Fire.

For all the four seasons: If the *chi* is black or white, you will be defeated completely within three days. The interpretation of blue, yellow or red *chi* in this instance remains a secret oral tradition. Also, if it rises from the hour of the Dragon to the hour of the Cock, you should be very careful. If it rises from the Dog to the Hare, then once again the interpretation remains shrouded in secrecy.

The *Chi* of Retreat

As seen in the picture overleaf, whether in a castle or a camp, if the smoke rises like a rod from the ridge of a roof, you should leave there as soon as possible. Therefore, it is called the *chi* of Retreat. If you stay long under this *chi*, you will meet a great disaster and a fire will likely occur.

In spring: if it rises during the Hours of the Tiger and the Hare, many people of the clan will die; if during the Hours of the Dragon, the Snake or the Horse, you will have a hardship caused by fire. There is a secret oral tradition for the hours of the Ram and the Monkey that remains unknown. If from the Hours of the Cockerel to the Rat, there will be a disaster caused by fire.

In summer: If it rises in the hour of the Dragon and lasts to the Ram, people will die; if it rises in the Hour of Monkey or Cockerel, there will be a disaster though fire. The interpretation for the hours from the Dog to the Rat remain unknown.

In autumn: There will be a disaster by fire if it rises in the Hours of the Horse to the Dog. If it is present in the hour of the Boar, the Rat or the Ox, many people will die. If present in the hour of the Dragon or the Snake, the interpretation is unknown.

In winter: If it comes in the hours from Cockerel to the Rat, many people will die, if from the Ox to the Horse then there is a secret oral tradition.

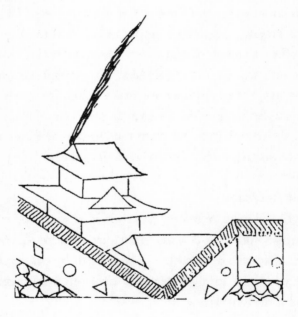

This *chi* is always of white and black. If it is blue, yellow or red, then it is not the *chi* of Retreat. The explanation for this remains a closely guarded secret.

The *Chi* of a Ninja or *Yato*

The *chi* you see as trailing smoke in the picture above is the sign of an enemy coming to conduct a night attack or of *shinobi* (ninja) coming to set fires. Therefore, it is called the *chi* of the *Yato* (night thieves). The attack will take place within three days if it can be seen from the hours from the Cockerel to the Rat. If it is from the hours from Ox to Monkey, then watch out for the attack that night. The same holds true all through the seasons. The colour of the *chi* should be yellow or black. If it is blue, red or white, be careful for the first fifteen days of the next month.

The *Chi* of a Fire Disaster

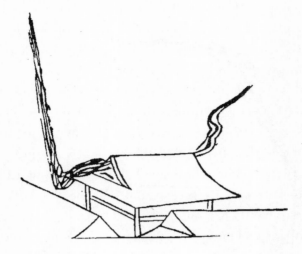

If you have *chi* from a building as seen in the picture above, a fire will break out within the clan, or you will be ruined by a fire which is set by the enemy, so it is called the Chi of a Fire Disaster.

In spring: If it is red or white, it is bad luck; if blue, yellow, or black then there is a secret oral tradition.

In summer: Black or red is bad luck; there is secret oral tradition for blue, yellow and white.

In autumn: Blue or red is bad luck; there is secret oral tradition for yellow, white and black.

All through the four seasons: If it rises during the hour of the Snake, the Horse, the Monkey, the Cockerel, the Dog or the Boar, you should be careful for three days; if from the Rat to the Dragon, then be careful for seven days.

The *Chi* of Raindrops

As seen in the picture opposite, the *chi* that does not rise up but looks like rain drops is called the *chi* of Raindrops. It is the *chi* of disaster and disease.

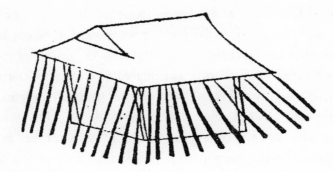

In spring: Red is a sign of disease, and black is for a fire disaster.
In summer: Red is for fire, while black is a sign of disease.
In autumn: Black is for disease while red is a sign of fire.
In winter: Red is for disease while black is for fire. If blue, yellow or white it means the house or clan will be destroyed. The tradition covering this interpretation remains secret.

The *Chi* of Flying Birds

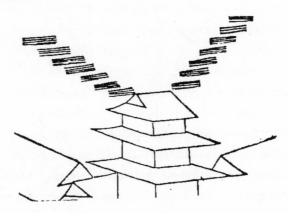

As seen in the picture above, the *chi* that looks like flying birds suggests that someone will betray you.
In spring: There is a secret oral tradition for if the *chi* rises from the hour of the Tiger to the Ram.

In summer: If it rises in the hours from the Horse to the Boar, retainers will betray a lord. There is a secret oral tradition for the hours from Rat to Snake.

In autumn: If it rises from the hour of the Dog to the Hare, retainers will betray a lord. There is a secret oral tradition if it rises in the hours from Dragon to Cockerel.

In winter: If it rises between the hour of the Cockerel and the Tiger, retainers will betray a lord. There is a secret oral tradition covering *chi* rising from the hour of the Hare to the Monkey.

The *Chi* of Death

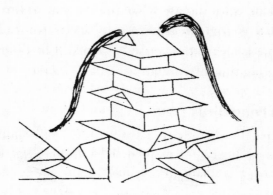

As seen in the picture, if the *chi* is hanging towards the ground, it is a *chi* that represents the lord being killed in battle. It is therefore called the *chi* of Death, and you should not go to war after seeing this *chi*.

In spring: If it is red, you should not fight on that day. If it is white, then do not battle within three days. If it is yellow, then the Hours of the Snake and the Horse are unlucky on that day. There is a secret oral tradition for blue or black.

In summer: If it is black, it means bad luck for thirty days. If it is yellow, it means bad luck only on that day. If white, it means bad luck from the hour of the Cockerel to the hour of the Rat. There is a secret oral tradition for blue or red.

In autumn: If blue, it means bad luck on that day; if yellow then it is bad luck within fifteen days. If red, then death will come after fifteen days. There is a secret oral tradition for white or black.

In winter: If blue it means bad luck on that day, while yellow means bad luck for thirty days; if white, ill fortune is met within three days. There is a secret oral tradition for red and black.

The *Chi* of Self-destruction

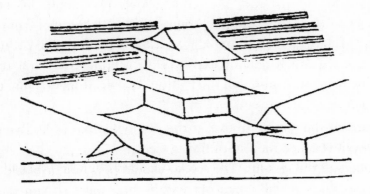

If *chi* is rising as seen in the picture then you will have arguments among your allies and your army will be defeated unexpectedly, so it is called the *Chi* of Self-destruction.

In spring: If it rises during the hour of the Snake or the Horse, it is a greater bad luck; if from the hour of the Ram to the Rat, there will be an argument but it will not lead to a defeat of the army. For the Hours of the Ox, the Tiger, the Hare and the Dragon there is a secret oral tradition.

In summer: If in the hours from Cockerel to Rat, it is greater bad luck; if from Ox to Horse, the army will not be defeated. There is an oral tradition if it appears in the hour of the Ram or the Monkey.

In autumn: From the Hours of the Rat to the Horse, it is greater bad luck; from the hour of the Ram or the Monkey, the army will not be defeated. There is an oral tradition for the hour of the Dog or Boar.

The *Chi* of Flying Geese

As seen in the picture above, if the *chi* looks like birds flying in the sky, it is called the Chi of Flying Geese.

Through all the seasons: The colour should be white or black. If it is seen a disaster will break out within three days, so you should be careful, however there is a secret oral tradition for this.

The *Chi* of a Loss of Souls

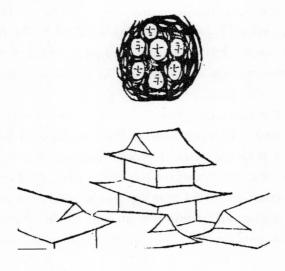

If the *chi* rising looks like human heads in a cloud, many people beneath it will be killed in a battle, so it is called Chi of a Loss of Souls. Most likely, it looks like white heads in red clouds.

In spring: If it rises from the hour of the Tiger to the Horse, the lord should be careful.

In summer: If from the hour of the Cockerel to the Rat, then the lord should be careful.

In autumn: If from the hour of the Cockerel to the Dog, the lord should be careful.

In winter: If from the Dog to the Snake, the lord should still be careful. There is a secret oral tradition for every case.

The *Chi* of the Colour of Death

If smoke rises as seen in the picture above it concerns the devastation of a camp, so it is called the Chi of the Colour of Death. Most likely, it is said that the lord will be killed in a battle. However, if the colour of the *chi* is in the Cycle of Creation when matched with the *chi* colour of the lord, he will not be killed even if he is injured. If it is the opposite and it is in a Cycle of Destruction, your army will be unexpectedly defeated within two days and the lord will be killed. If it rises from the hour of the Rat to the Dragon, there will be a fire.

The *Chi* of the Cucurbit

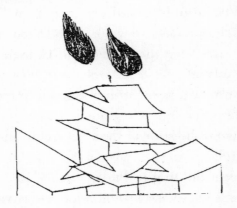

The side that has *chi* rising as seen in the picture may be defeated by a night attack. If it is blue, you should be careful during the hour of the Rat on that day. If yellow, then be careful during the hour of the Ox. If red, then look to the hours from Boar to Rat. There is a secret oral tradition for white and black.

The *Chi* of Two Birds

This *chi* implies you may end up with mutual destruction and that your army may be too excitable. If it rises from the hour of the Hare to the Horse, you will not win in battle but the lord will also not be in danger. If 'birds' like these are 'perching' or have 'fallen' from the hour of the Ram to the Cockerel, the lord should be careful.

The *Chi* of Ruin

As seen in the picture above, it is a *chi* rising like a gathering of cut hair between heaven and the castle. If the or tip of the *chi* is pointing to the ground the lord will be destroyed, so it is called the Chi of Ruin. You should be careful. If it is black, disaster will occur within twenty-one days. If white, there is a secret oral tradition.

The *Chi* of the End of Life

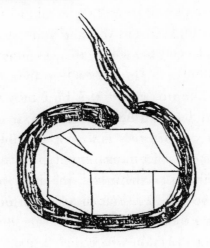

If *chi* is hugging the ground vigorously and encircling the quarters like in the picture above, the lord will kill himself through *seppuku*. It is therefore called the *chi* of the End of Life. However, if the colour is in the Cycle of Destruction when compared to the lord's *chi* colour, there can be no change to the event even if you pray; if it is in the Cycle of Creation when compared to the lord's *chi* colour, then you should pray to the local guardian or to Heaven. A small, secret oral tradition is kept for this.

The *Gunpo Jiyoshu* manual also states but does not illustrate the following:

The *Chi* of Annihilation

If there is no *chi* rising on the camp or castle and no 'power' can be felt from the people, like the aftermath of a big storm, a terrible thing will happen within three days. If there is no *chi* coming from your army or your enemy's army and colour is not emanating, then this is the *chi* of Reconciliation. If the colours for both armies are emanating there will be a battle of annihilation so that the both lords will die on each other's swords.

Tips on Defence

If someone comes and talks to you and you have a bitter taste in your mouth, you should know that the person is going to deceive and kill you.

Whether in a camp or castle, if a bird calls three times, you should be all right. If you hear more calls, it is bad luck. You should throw up your defences as soon as possible and have night patrols or other, more strict measures put in place.

When stars are near to the moon, the army on the same side as the stars will be defeated. You should send out a night attack against your enemy if this is the case.

Do not go to the direction where there are no stars. Also, on a cloudy night, do not head for the direction where the clouds are shining.

The Luck of Watch Fires

If a watch fire has twin pointed flames and is whitish in colour, it is a bad sign.

Even if the watch fire is big, if it has no distinct core in its flames but is just burning feebly, it is bad luck. Alternatively, even if it is not a big fire but has a core which is rising upright, then this is good luck.

If black smoke rises from the edge of the watch fire and obscures the fire itself, it is called the *chi* of Conflict and is a greater bad luck. You will be defeated severely on the next day if this is the case.

The Luck of Flags

When being given a flag on the way to battle, the receiver should not receive it palm-up but should have his hand palm-down. Receiving with the right hand and turning to the left is bad luck. You should receive it palm-down with the left hand and turn to the right; this assures greater good luck.

If an arrow pierces a flag on your side, attack the enemy quickly so you can defeat them. If an arrow shot from your side pierces a flag of the enemy, the person should unstring the bow immediately and you should abandon the battle on that day.

Bringing an enemy flag to your side is a bad action. If you need to, cut it into three, fold the pieces and bury them. Use the ritual of *kuji kiri* and pray on that site.

Understanding the Luck of a Flag in the Wind

勝つ事眼前なり。

If it turns like this, you will win after a long battle.

If it turns like this, your victory is close at hand.

If it turns around like this, you should not give battle until the *chi* has changed.

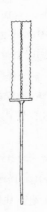

If it is upright like this (flying directly up above the banner pole), you will not fight during that day. If it moves toward your side it is half good luck, but if it turns toward the enemy go to battle immediately as the enemy will lose.

If the flag is floating away from the pole as in the above picture, the direction the wind comes from is not bad luck; it is the other direction, of no wind, that is of ill luck.

The Good or Bad Luck of Dogs' Howling

There is also good or bad luck attributed to the way a dog comes around the camp and howls. If the season and the direction are in a Cycle of Destruction then it is bad luck, while if they are in a Cycle of Creation it is good luck.

The Twenty-Eight Lunar Mansions

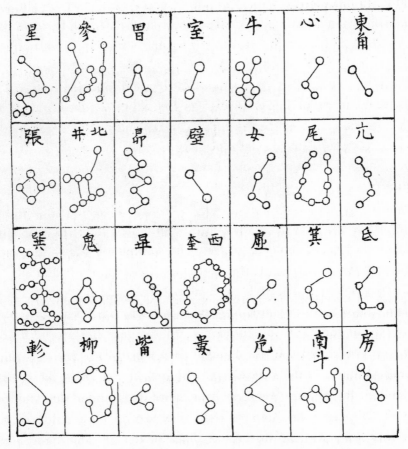

A table of the twenty-eight lunar mansions from the *Book of Ninja* (1676).

The Japanese imported the concept of the twenty-eight lunar mansions; these are twenty-eight positions in the night sky that are identified by twenty-eight different constellations. When a person plots them all, the night sky is divided into twenty-eight divisions, like looking out from the centre of an orange. When the moon rises in 'X' mansion, it is said to be in the mansion of 'X'. This is how they used to plot the lunar month, and in connection with the solar calendar they mapped out the year (in quite a complex way).

The Star of Defeat

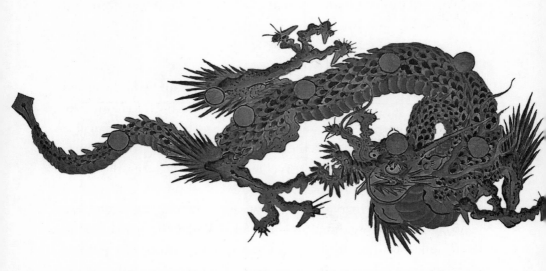

The constellation Ursa Major in the form of a dragon, taken from the secret scrolls of Mubyoshi-Ryu. The full teachings can be found in *The Lost Samurai School*.

Hagun is the evil star, or the star of defeat. In the constellation Ursa Major it is the star Alkaid, the one at the very end of the 'handle'. In military matters, if an army was under this star or in the direction of this star then they would be considered to be in a negative position and a place of defeat. This had to be balanced with aspects of real tactical advantage, but this was a discussion between the *gunposha* (normal tactician) and the *gunbaisha* (esoteric tactician) and a warlord would set up position on the advice of both.

12

DARK CURIOSITIES AND SUPERSTITIONS OF ANCIENT JAPAN

The following section will take a look into the dark heart of Japanese superstitions, those elements on the fringe of mainstream belief that create a web of fear and force people to counter the unknown with ritual actions and trinkets of protection. It will provide those short stories that will fill five minutes by the fire with a slice of horror.

Plants

On the Ryukyu Island chain, the Japanese climbing fern (*Lygodium Japonicum*), a form of creeper plant, is used to capture evil things. You can wear them as headdresses or amulets or you can make wreaths of them and place them around your home or objects to help keep the area pure. The belief is that the tangling nature of the plant will entangle the spirits of the dead or evil entities within it, ensnaring them.

Also, the use of a loop made from straw and maiden grass (*Miscanthus sinensis*) or the pointed leaf of the Pandanus tree (*Pandanus odoratissimus*) will help purify a person or food offerings. It should be tied to a person or left with offerings at shrines.

Mountains

Mountains have always been sacred to many, and Japan is no different. In its most basic form, Japanese mountain worship can be divided into three sections.

I

Conical dormant volcanos. The sleek sides of these majestic monoliths are worshiped by many, and the most famous of these – perhaps one of the most famous mountains on the planet – is Mt Fuji. Alongside Fuji, there is also Mt Chokai, Mt Taisen and Mt Kaimon, all holy mountains in their own right. These mountains are worshipped by many, but they are often venerated by sailors and fishermen in particular as the place where the gods or spirits of navigation reside.

II

As a water source. Mountains are also worshipped as the source of water for the local areas. Two terms come into play here: *Yama no kami* (spirit of the mountain) and *Ta no kami* (spirit of the rice paddy). These two spirits are thought to dwell in the mountains and the fields around the mountain (sometimes they are combined and sometimes the same spirit moves from mountain to field). Their task is to bring water and promote bounty in agriculture.

III

As a place of the dead. A mountain has its base at ground level and yet reaches to the heavens. Therefore, in the minds of the old Japanese it is quite literally a 'stairway to heaven'. This means that some mountains are the place where spirits of the dead dwell and ascend to heaven or simply make their next home. Often mountains or islands will appear in *banka*, which are Japanese funeral songs/poems in which a family express their lamentation for the dead.

One dark legend about mountains is the story of Mt Ibuki in Omi. Upon its peak lived a malevolent deity, but the samurai Yamato Dake ventured deep into the mountain intending to kill the demon-god. On his way up he saw a pure white snake (sometimes a boar) and thought of this as a good omen, a message from the gods; however, it was in fact the evil god leading him to his doom. The samurai walked into a malicious mist that drained him of his energy and made him appear drunk. He was only saved from death by drinking from a holy well on the mountain, which brought him back to his senses.

There is the tale of Utsurai Sayo, who summoned demons, devils and spirits on a mountain and bound them with reed. Having magically bound them, he left them under a peach tree as food for tigers. Because of this, a continuing tradition (mainly in China) is to take figurines made from peach tree wood and to tie them up with reeds on the last day of the Chinese year; this is done for protection against evil spirits.

Once a man was walking in the mountains when he saw a robe of feathers hanging from a tree, and when he took the robe a figure came out and asked for the robe back; the figure was in fact an angel and needed the robe in order to fly. The man, returning the robe, watched as the angel flew into the sky and performed a dance above Mt Fuji.

The Horse River

There is a river called Banyugawa (*Ba* means horse). It is said that the shogun was attending the opening ceremony of a bridge which crossed this river when all of a sudden there was an evil squall, and in the thunder and darkness came ghosts and spirits, making the shogun's horse bolt into the river, where it drowned.

The Violet Well

One day a lady named Shinge was looking at violet flowers near a well when a snake attacked her. Her handmaidens threw a basket at the snake and it retreated. A young man who came by was skilled in medicine and helped to save her. Shinge grew better but then fell back into illness because she could not marry the handsome stranger who had saved her. It turned out that he was called Yoshisawa and was from the *Eta* class in Japan, the 'unclean' class. Being the daughter of a lord, she could not marry him; her father forbade it. Upon hearing this news she threw herself into the Violet Well, and her ghost is known to cry out on stormy nights with her love of Yoshisawa.

The Ghost in the Well

Okiku was a servant girl who broke an expensive plate from a set. The mistress of the house was greatly displeased and imprisoned her. Filled with sorrow, the girl escaped from her cell and jumped into the well, killing herself. She is often depicted as crawling out of the well with plates in her hands.

The above two stories show how many old Japanese tales make it on to the silver screen; indeed, some of those films end up being shown to Western audiences. The most famous example is *The Ring*, where the central horrific figure is that of a ghost from a well.

The Soul of the Mirror

There was a priest called Matsumura who took up residence in a haunted house – it had a well that was very unlucky and had dragged many people to their death. One day a servant was found dead in the well, and it was a man people knew would not commit suicide. This event made Matsumura take particular interest in the well. One night a woman called Yayori came to him and said that she was the soul of a mirror that was in the well. She said that she had lived in the well by order of an evil demon who had made her entice people to their deaths but had no choice in the matter, and now that the demon was gone she would like to make a request of the master of the house. She asked him to look into the well and find her mirror and bring it out from the depths. The next day he had well cleaners go into the well, and, just as she said, the mirror was found. Upon the back was the name Yayori. He had the mirror polished and placed in a box. The spirit of the mirror came to Matsumura again and said that she was distantly connected to the current shogun, Yoshimasa. She told him to leave the house for it was about to be washed away in a flood and to take her back to the shogun. Moving the very next day, the priest visited the shogun and was rewarded with funding for a new temple and other gifts.

Well Cleaners

Japan used to have well cleaners. Wells had to be cleaned once a year to avoid incurring the wrath of Sujin-sama, the god of wells. Two fish would be put in the well to eat the grime and keep it clean and would be brought out of the well each year when it was given its yearly scrub.

Toenails

One fun superstition is the concept of not clipping your nails at night, the superstition arising from a play on words: 'Yo-tsume', meaning 'night and nails', also has the phonetic meanings 'shortening your life' and 'to die early'.

Numbers

As we have the unlucky number thirteen, the Japanese have the numbers four and nine. These are considered unlucky numbers in Japan because of the sounds they make. The number four (四 or *Shi*) has the same sound for the word death. The number nine (九 or *Ku*) has the same sound as the word for pain. Therefore, you will find that sometimes a building may or may not have a fourth or ninth floor or that someone may not give you four or nine pieces of something, such as cakes or sweets. However, this is a fading custom as Japanese culture gives way to the Western traditions.

Shamanic beliefs show that seven is a powerful number. On the Ryukyu Island chain, there is a belief that there are seven founding siblings, seven souls in the human body and forty-nine bones in a human. Post-mortem rites happen every seven days until the forty-ninth day, and worship of the dead happens in the seventh lunar month. However, others believe that seven is unlucky and that numbers including a seven are negative.

Internal Bleeding

On the battlefield, a samurai may suffer from internal bleeding; to counter this they had a strange recipe to help stop the blood flow. You could either drink the blood of a grey horse, or, if the blood was not available, you could boil the dung of a grey horse, mix it in water and drink it.

Shells

On the Ryukyu Island chain of Japan it is a shamanistic tradition to hang a spider conch shell (*Lambis chiragra*) on your front door to ward off spirits that adopt different shapes.

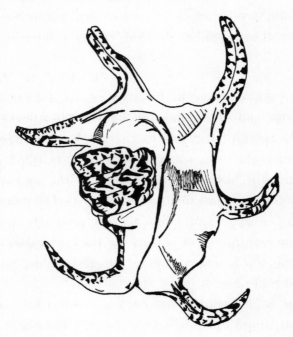

New Year
'*Ichi-Fuji, Ni-Taka, San-Nasubi*' is a Japanese memory hook which represents a superstition that is centred on the New Year. It translates to 'Mt Fuji, a hawk, an eggplant'. Old wisdom holds that it is good luck to dream of these three things on the first or second night of the New Year, dreaming of Mt Fuji being of the greatest good luck.

The Dead in the North
Never sleep with your head to the north as the dead are laid with their heads to the north. From the early twentieth century onwards, Japan moved from burials to cremation; now, when bodies are awaiting cremation they are placed with the head to the north.

Hide Your Thumbs
When you see a hearse, hide your thumbs inside of your clenched fists. Your thumbs represent your parents, and also under the nail of a thumb was believed to be a gateway of the spirit; thus you should guard it so that the taint of death will not invade you.

Parade of Demons
The Hyakkiyagyo is a famous scroll of *yokai* monsters of Japan, but it takes its name from an event. The event concerns the dead and other such things marching through the streets of Kyoto during the night. The name loosely means 'procession of one hundred demons at night'.

Rebirth
If a person dies, you can write their name in ink on the left hand of the corpse and pray that they will come back in the next life in a better position. When reborn, their next body should have a birthmark of what was written on the body and

the only way it can be removed is by rubbing clay from the grave of the last incarnation upon it.

Hell

The concept of Hell in Japanese is a difficult one to approach, and though it has not been ignored here it has been kept at arm's length. The reason for this is that Hell is a concept predominantly brought via Buddhism, and therefore any talk of Hell in Japanese culture is heavily influenced by Indian and Chinese thought. For this short book on Japan, it is enough to understand that Japan had its own idea of Hell and that several versions existed:

Jigoku   The archetypal Hell of pain and punishment
Yomi   The Shinto version of Hell (somewhat milder)
Ahtata (Sanskrit)   A hell where the lips are frozen
Ahbaba (Sanskrit)   A hell where the tongue is frozen
Pundarika (Sanskrit)   A hell known as 'White Lotus' because the bones there are bleached by the cold and look like a vast array of white lotuses on a pond. (A separate but interesting connection between lotuses and hell can be seen by the figure of Kwannon, who went to the lowest section of Hell and shouted '*Amitofo!*', at which point lotuses floated down through Hell, causing the very foundations of this under-realm to shake, releasing scores of damned souls and creatures.)

The Regent of Hell is Yemma (pronounced Emma in Japanese), who has many aides to help him. In hell this regent may make a a soul face the reflecting mirror (the *tabari no kagami*) which shows the reality of the true nature of an individual's soul back to them. The Regent of Hell and his minions are said to be fed molten copper every eight hours, and some versions have the regent with three eyes, holding a sceptre made from a holy head. In the first and seventh months, a festival was held for the Regent of Hell and his apprentices were given the day off.

The River of Hell or the River Styx has its counterpart in Japanese mythology and is called the River of Three Roads, Sanzu no Kawa or Sai-no-kawara. On the banks of this river there is a hag called Shozuka Baba who is 16 (sometimes 60) feet tall and has large eyes. She robs the dead of their clothing and hangs the garments up on trees. She does this with the aid of her consort, Ten Datsuba, to gain the 3 *rin* payment required. However, her life is not all roses, as the deity Jizo is constantly there to protect children from her scavenging. People of a bad nature are led to Hell by Kakure Zato, the blind guide. At times the children in Hell build small towers of stones; the demons knock them down, which makes the laughing children cry and run for the protection of Jizo.

Mummies

On Mt Yudono there existed a strange sect of people who are linked to the term *Sokushinbutsu*, which refers to a Buddhist practice involving self-mummification. The idea is simple but the execution is difficult. An aspiring future mummy will start a harsh regime of frequent fasting, intensive religious routine and mountain pilgrimages. They then move on to *Mokijiki*, which is the premise of only eating food from trees, such as nuts, berries, tree bark and pine needles. This diet is steadily reduced until it leads to literal starvation over a period of around 2,000 days. The overall plan is to reduce the body to an almost skeletal state and dry out the internal organs while alive. Would-be mummies have to drink from special wells which sometimes have naturally occurring chemicals that help to kill bacteria in the digestive tract so that rot will not set in. When the aspirant reaches the final stage they can be buried in a type of grave with a tube for air, still chanting and ringing bells. When their chants fail and the bells fall silent, the monks above know that the would-be mummy has died; the monks then wait an extended period of time before they retrieve the body. If successful, the body will be dry and without decay and they will thus have achieved sainthood, allowing them to be used by the shrine as an object of worship. The candidate themselves will have attained pure enlightenment and should then be released from the cycle of rebirth. However, not all make it. Many people died without success in the attempt; it is said that you can still see certain marker stones which mark the areas where many have failed this test and died.

If you would like to see these mummified remain today you can visit them at Churenji Temple, where the remains of Tesumonkai Same and Hommyokai Shonin are held, and Kaikoji Temple in the town of Sakata, which holds the bodies of Shinnyokai Dainichibo and two other unknown mummies.

The Emperor's Lost Tombs

Much like Western mysteries over the graves of Robin Hood and King Arthur, there are numerous tombs or burial sites in Japan that claim to contain lost emperors. One is said to hold Emperor Antoku, who reigned between 1180 and 1185 and went missing in a battle between the Taira and Minamoto clans. Similarly, the location of the remains of Emperor Chokei, who reigned between 1368 and 1383, are also 'lost'. When you travel Japan, you may therefore come upon a holy site claiming to be the last resting place of one of these rulers. However, take it with a pinch of salt as there are many more who also claim this.

Stones of Japan

From traditional gardens to Shinto shrines, Japan has an adoration of stone sites, from its rich Stone Age culture to burial mounds from a time long forgotten. Legends survive today of archers who thought they had struck a tiger but in fact shot and split a stone in two, or even famed swordsmen who cracked open vast slabs with a single stroke.

One lesser-known story is that of the Death Stone, told in the play *Sessho Sekki*. In this tale we see the jewel maiden – a fox in disguise – take the shape of a stone, and anyone who looks at her instantly dies. However, her demonic and cursed stone form was destroyed when the holy man Genno Osho prayed towards it, shattering it into a thousand pieces. Chamberlin translated the following poem on the subject:

> The Death-Stone stands on Nasu's moor
> Through winter snows and summer heat
> The moss grows grey upon its sides
> But the fowl demon haunts it yet

> Chill blows the blast, the owl's sad choir
> Hoots hoarsely through the moaning pines
> Among the low chrysanthemums
> The skulking fox, the jackal whines
> As over the moor the autumn light declines

Another myth in the world of rock is that of the *Crying Stone*. In the fourteenth century, a pregnant wife was waiting for her soldier husband to return from war. Tired of waiting, she went to find him in the province of Musashi but on the way was raped on the road; the rapist left her for dead. Lying there, she gave birth to a boy but died in labour, and along came a holy man – Jizo Bo Satsu – who took the baby and raised him. When he was old enough, the boy tracked down the murderer (who was boasting of his deeds) and took bloody revenge. The spot of the rape became the birthplace of the Crying Stone, Yonaki Ishi. It can be heard crying aloud in the wind and rain.

The Japanese Heracles

Ariwara no Narihira is a legendary twelfth-century warrior who charged into Hell, defeated the 'Hag of Three Roads' (Sodzuka no Baba) at the River into Hell, had afternoon tea (well, refreshments) with the Regent of Hell, swam near to China with a shark under each arm, and, in classic Heracles style, pulled up a tree and used it as a giant club. A man to be reckoned with.

Jikininki

Muso Kokushi was a Zen priest who was travelling through the land of Mino when he lost his way. Finding a small hermit retreat on a hilltop, he asked for sanctuary for the evening. However, the man inside forbade him to enter, saying that a village was in the valley and that he should go there. Moving on, Muso came to the village and was welcomed, but the villagers were leaving that very night as someone had died and it was their custom to leave the corpse alone and move out of the village each time someone passed on. Muso, telling them he was a priest, declared that he would stay and tend to the body; the villagers told him to be wary. Later that night, in the darkest hours, a vast and vague shape came into the room, lifting and devouring the corpse. When it had finished, it retreated back into the darkness. Muso, having survived the night, left the village and returned to the hut on the hill where he was refused lodgings. The man inside greeted him again, but this time told him that he was ashamed because Muso had seen his true form – he was the monster who ate the corpses of the dead. He was a *jikininki*, a man-devouring monster, cursed owing to the greed he displayed in his human life.

The Corpse-Eating Samurai

There was once a woman who was allowed to pick her own husband. She declared that she would marry any samurai who would pass a test she set, but on their word of honour they would never divulge the secrets of the test. Many brave and rich samurai came and went but none would speak of her test, nor would they attempt it. Then a poor, low-ranking samurai armed only with his sword took up the challenge. The woman instructed him to meet her in the cemetery that night. When he arrived the lady was dressed in white and digging up the corpse of a child. When she reached the coffin she tore it open and ripped away an arm of the dead baby, starting to devour it and offering the other arm to the samurai. As he sat down and started to eat the arm, the lady exclaimed that she had found her brave samurai and that they would be married. In a pleasant twist to the story, when the samurai ate the arm, it tasted sweet and was a delight to savour.

The Willow Tree Woman

A samurai from Noto named Tomotada was travelling through the mountains to another province on a diplomatic mission when he was waylaid by a snowstorm and sought shelter in a cottage. The hosts had their daughter serve him, and the samurai fell in love with the country girl. In the hope that she would have a good life with the samurai, the parents presented her to him. The samurai, still on the mission for his lord, hid her and her beauty for fear that the lord he was visiting would interfere. However, the lord saw the truth of their love and allowed them to marry, even though she was of common birth. They returned to Tomotada's home province and lived a short while, but one day, struck with pain in her side, she called him over and said that their life together had come to an end and that she would soon be dead. Nonetheless, she reassured him that they would be together in the next life. Faced with his disbelief, she was forced to tell the truth. She was no human; in fact, she was the spirit of a willow tree, as were her parents, and at that very moment her tree must have been struck by an axe. After she died, the samurai journeyed back to the cottage where he had met her and there, next to the cottage, were three willow trees, cut down and dead. The woman's name was Aoyagi, which means 'green willow'.

The Samurai and His Tree-wife

There was once a samurai who wanted to cut down a willow tree in his garden, but a samurai of the same neighbourhood said that the tree had a soul and he should not kill the tree. He offered to buy the tree and replant it in his own garden. The soul of the tree, glad of this, appeared as a beautiful woman and married the man. They gave birth to a son and there was love in the family. However, one day the lord demanded the tree for a wooden beam in a new monastery, and no matter how much the samurai pleaded with the lord, the tree was doomed. His wife died when the tree was cut down, leaving their son behind. No matter how many men were used to haul the tree, it would not budge. The son came over and took the tree by a branch like it was a hand and the tree got to its 'feet' and danced to the place where it was cut as a beam.

The Winter Cherry Tree

Sakura or Japanese cherry blossoms are famous, but most special in Japan is the single cherry blossom that flowers on the sixteenth day of the first lunar month (normally around February) in full glory and during the season of snow.

The story is as follows: a samurai had grown very old and outlived his children, and all he had left was one old cherry tree, withered and old but precious as a reminder of the golden years of his life. One year the tree died, giving flowers no more. Devastated, he decided that only one action could take place. He laid out a white cloth on the floor and gave his life for the tree so that it might bloom again. Cutting open his stomach, he died as his blood poured into the roots and the tree burst into life once more. It was the sixteenth day of the first lunar month and the tree blossomed in snowfall – something that would never happen naturally.

The Tree on Mt Oki

The mountain Oki-yama has a temple upon it to the god Fudo, and the priest Yenoki had been the guardian of the temple statue for nearly twenty years. However, he had not once seen the statue because only the high priest could see it. One day the door was open and he looked inside; at that instant, Yenoki was struck blind in one eye and cursed to live as a *Tengu* for a year. After that year his spirit was put into a great tree on top of the mountain. This tree became a beacon and object of prayer during storms, and it is said that if you are in a storm nearby and you pray to the tree and flames are seen in the tree then the storm will abate. On one part of the mountain was a village where the people were said to be without morals, conducting all manner of sexual offences. During the *bon-odori* dances for the dead, the youth of the village would copulate with anyone and their actions were considered improper. Yenoki changed his guise into that of a handsome youth and lured young girls out of the village area with his looks, but then he tied them to trees until they repented. A representative of the village went to Yenoki's great tree and pleaded with the spirit. Yenoki appeared to him and said that he may go fetch the women who were tied to the trees and return them to their village, as now they will lead great lives and instruct the others on virtue.

The Haunted Futon

The Futon of Tottori is a story of two boys who owned only a futon bed after their mother died. They sold the futon to raise some money, but soon their landlord came and threw them out into the street. Freezing in the snow and with no one to help, they clung desperately to each other but deep in the snow they died. The futon, with its new owner, began to emit strange sounds of boys crying, at which point the new and horrified owner gave it to a temple to take care of the spirits of the dead.

The Price of Good Health
In an ancient court there was a prince who fell ill. A high-ranking but elderly woman found a cure, but the cure was made from the blood of children who were born in a particular month. The story continues that one night a traveller passed by the house where the woman killed the children. Entering the house, he was warned not to go in a specific room; however, as it is with tales of mystery, he opened the sliding doors to reveal a room of bones and children's remains. It is also said that the prince and the elderly woman ate the dead.

The Master Wizard
Kakubaku (or in Chinese Kwoh P'oh) was a wizard and philosopher who is said to have mastered ancient secrets and possessed nine bound books on philosophy and Taoist magic. Legend says he died in AD 324, and he is normally shown crossing the sea with a demon on his back – presumably under his control.

Shadow Destroyer
This man was a wizard of extreme ability. It is said that he destroyed his own shadow and could divide his body into sections and that he could live in the centre of any inferno. The king decided to test this ability and ordered a pile of wood bundles to be set alight to create a raging column of fire, challenging the man to enter. After he disappeared from view, the king and the onlookers waited till the flames died; to their surprise the man was simply sat reading. He got up and brushed the ash off his arms.

The Lost Geisha

When the samurai lost power during the restoration of the emperor, many families had to suffer poverty and lacked work. One samurai family fell to ruin, and having sold all their belongings they were left with nothing. Remembering that they had buried their father with his sword, which had gold mounts on it, they dug up his grave, took the gold off the sword and replaced it with iron and sold the gold. However, the money this provided did not last and the elder daughter was forced to become a geisha to provide for the family. This daughter was Kimiko, who in the end became a famous geisha. She grew famously wealthy, and supported her family so that her sister could get educated as a proper samurai child should. However, in the end Kimiko disappeared and all searches for her failed; she had run away and was never seen again.

Hikohichi Omori and the Demon Witch

Hikohichi, a samurai warrior, came to a stream or small river and found a beautiful woman at the edge, waiting for someone to help her across. The samurai, gallant, took her upon his back and started to cross. As he moved through the water, he looked down to the surface of the stream and saw, to his horror, not the reflection of a beautiful young woman, but a demonic crone on his back. Immediately he threw the devil-woman down, drew his longsword and cut her through. An alternative version has the woman not as a demon but a spy, the sister of the great samurai Kusunoki Masashige, sent for vengeance. This story holds that she was in fact wearing a demon mask and was there to assassinate Hikohichi.

Yuki Chi

The king of Hang Yu in China is said to have had the most beautiful wife in all the land. However, this became a curse for the king, as while he was surrounded on all sides by his enemies and the land was under invasion, he refused to leave her side. No one could persuade him to leave her and take his armies to war, so the nation was in turmoil. To save the land she retired to her rooms and cut her own throat, leaving the lord free to save the people. Sad and angry, the king rode out with the head of his beautiful damsel tied it to the saddle of his horse. The tale gets sadder, as when the horse was crossing the Black River it saw the head reflected in the water and threw off the king. The enemy rushed upon him but, the king quickly committed suicide so that he could not be captured. And so the wife and the king lay dead in the River Black – well, at least her head, anyway.

Ghost Dog

A pious couple who lived next to a delinquent couple had a dog named Shiro who had the ability to find buried gold. The neighbours, trying and failing to use the dog, killed it in anger. But this did not stop Shiro, who returned as a helpful spirit and told his master that if he cut a certain tree down and carved from it the base section of a rice pounder then any rice placed in it would turn to little golden nuggets. Doing so, the family became rich all the more. The delinquent neighbours tried to use the mortar but found it failed them and only produced filth, so they burned it. From here the legend extends to the male of the good couple venturing out on more gold- and prize-finding journeys, but he always stays pious, resulting in the evil neighbours mending their horrible ways.

Hangonko – The Spirit in the Smoke

This legend is the foundation of the Japanese Noh play *Sendai Hagi*. Date Tsunamune, a prince and warlord of the Sengoku period, saw Miura Yatakao, a beauty of rare quality, and coveted her. His power was so great that he ordered her to journey to his distant castle. Upon hearing this, she gave incense to her lover, a *ronin* (leaderless samurai) called Shimasa Jusaburo, and told him that if she should die then he should light it and see her face in the smoke. Upon getting to the castle, Date Tsunamune gave Yatakao a choice: be his lover or die. She chose death, and it is said that her lover used the incense to commune with her, seeing her spirit in the smoke.

The Lover of 100 Nights

Ono no Matchi told her lover that if he visited 100 nights in a row in a show of devotion then she would marry him. He came for ninety-nine nights, but on the 100th he was nowhere to be seen. The next morning it turned out that he had frozen to death trying to make it to his lover in a blizzard.

Washing Away Sin

In the province of Echizen, when a woman died in childbirth people would write their name on a square section of white cloth in black ink. They would find a place near a stream and put four sticks of equal size in the ground in a square layout. After this, they would tie the four corners of the cloth to the sticks so the name was facing upwards to the sky (imagine a miniature table with long legs, the cloth facing the sky). Then, a ladle was placed next to the stream and when each passer-by walked past they would ladle one portion of water over the name on the cloth, letting the water seep through. The magic is that by the time the ink has worn off, all of the 'sins' of the woman will have gone and she will find paradise.

The Curse of the Heike and Genji Clans

The Genpei War was a twelfth-century conflict between the Heike clan (sometimes Taira) and the Minamoto clan (sometimes Genji). Legend says that one species of crab, the Heikegani, is actually an embodiment of the lost souls of the Battle of Dan no Ura in 1185, where the Heike army drowned. This legend also extends itself to a battle between fireflies which is recorded as Genji Botaru. The larger species of firefly is the Minamoto clan and the smaller ones are the Heike and they are re-enacting the famous battle, cursed to repeat it for all time. People who drowned in this war are thought to be in spirit form at the bottom of the ocean, baling the vast expanse of water with bottomless buckets, again cursed for eternity.

Another legend says that a warrior from this conflict wrote a poem and killed himself at the battle – he was seventy-five years old. After dying he turned into a firefly. The poem reads:

> All the dead,
> Trees that do not bloom,
> How poor the fruit harvest is.

The Dragon and the Bell

Once upon a time, a young girl was shown affection by a monk. This affection was returned with a deep and addictive love, and when the girl came of age the love turned into sexual obsession. Being devout, the monk refused her many times, until her love turned to vengeance and hatred. The woman tried spells and charms and witchcraft to get her way or to take revenge on his slights, none of which worked. In the end she turned to deep magic and waited for the monk to walk under the temple bell, a 5-foot-high bronze dome. As he walked past she touched the superstructure and supports of the bell, causing it to crash down with a mighty ringing and encase the monk. The monk was now trapped inside the bell, and the woman, wearing a demonic face, shifted into the form of a dragon and jumped upon the bell, coiling around it. With her tail she used a T-shaped hammer to ring on the bell repeatedly while her entire body erupted into flames, forming a blazing prison. When she left, the rest of the monks moved the bell and found only pure white ash where the pious monk had been. On the air they heard one finial prayer to Buddha.

The Woman and the Bell of Miidera

There was a great bell in the Temple of Miidera that sounded sweet and was as shiny as a mirror. However, no woman was allowed to touch the bell lest it lose its holiness. One woman, so curious of this bell, dressed herself a man and went to it; captivated by its reflective surface, she touched the bell. Instantly a hole burned through the bronze and all the silver platting came away, ruining the bell forever.

Another story of the bell of Miidera is of Benki, the famous warrior strongman of Japan who appears many times in Japanese folklore. He stole the bell and carried it to another temple. However, when fixed in its new belfry and struck, the bell simply cried that it wanted to return to Miidera and was therefore returned.

The Revenge of Kanshiro

There was a devout man called Kanshiro who had always made pilgrimages to holy places. He was nearing the end of his life and thought that he could make one more to the shrine at Ise. His village came together and gave him a great bag of money that they had collected for him to give to the temple as an offering. On the way to Ise he stopped at a village to rest and asked Jimpachi, an innkeeper to safeguard his money. The innkeeper did so and all was well. Kanshiro took back possession of the bag and went on his way. Further on his trip he opened the bag to check on the money but found no money there but only rocks of the same weight. Outraged, he headed back to the village and demanded that the money be returned, but Jimpachi this time was a different man – he was rude and cruel, and threw him out of the village. The old man returned to his native village and sold his house to pay everyone back the money they had given to the shrine.

Old man Kanshiro was now homeless and wandered the streets. He found his way back to Jimpachi's inn and discovered that Jimpachi had a new house and was wealthy. The old man begged and begged for the money to be returned but to no avail, so he laid a curse on the cruel Jimpachi. Kanshiro died on the village boundary as he was being thrown out. It was here that the curse of Kanshiro came to life! A local priest had cremated the old man and given him a grave and said the correct rites, but one night thousands of fireflies came from the grave and flew into Kimpachi's room. They hounded him and beat against his mosquito net. People came to see, and even though they struck at the fireflies, killing hundreds of them, thousands replaced them until the net collapsed under the weight. For weeks they flew in and out of cruel Jimpachi's mouth and ears, and for weeks he was tormented, eventually dying. At the instant of his death, the fireflies all flew away, never to be seen again. It was said this was the vengeance of Kanshiro.

Japanese Revenge

While the above is a story of revenge from the grave, taking revenge was in fact seen as a duty in Japan. One famous example is the story of the forty-seven *ronin*, who planned for a year or more before killing a court official after their *daimyo* (lord) was compelled to commit *seppuku*. Hearn describes instances of Japanese vengeance where a person would walk 50 miles in a day, kill ten men in under a minute and then turn the sword upon themselves. It is said by Hearn that there was even a fellow who had his own headstone prepared before he went on a mission of vengeance.

The Chinese Bell of 100 Leagues

In old China a lord wished to have a bell that could sound for one hundred *ri* (roughly equivalent to 100 leagues, or 250 miles) and so he had his smiths mix many metals, including gold and silver, to make the perfect bell. However, the metals would not mix and the great bell cracked and failed when its mould cooled. It was crafted again but it split. The bell caster was told that if it did not work again then his head would roll. So, as the people watched the third casting of the bell and the molten metals bubbled and boiled, the daughter of the smith leapt into the red-hot liquid and cried out that her death was for the sake of her father. The bell caster tried to jump after her but was held back. When tempers (and the bell) had cooled, the mould was taken off; before them lay a pristine bell which, when struck, echoed more than one hundred *ri* and was perfect in form.

Oshichi and the Love of Fire

Another love story is of Oshichi, a greengrocer's daughter. She had stayed at Kichijoji temple to shelter from a fire, and while there she fell in love with a samurai. However, she and he father soon returned home, separating the lovers. Dying of heartbreak, she racked her brain to find a way to see the samurai, then in a moment of inspiration thought that she would burn down another building in the village so that her father would go back to the temple to pray and take refuge. She commenced the deed but was caught in the act and arrested as the building burned to the ground. As she was only thirteen she was not meant to be given the death sentence; however, she had lied at the temple, telling the samurai and others that she was sixteen. Because of this she was given an arsonists' execution: she was burnt alive. She has become a warning to anyone connected with fire, and she even had an effect on the birth rate in Japan in 1966 – but that will be explained later.

The Story of Okatsu

There is a shrine in Kurosaka that is famous for its ghosts. One day a woman named Okatsu had a bet with her friends and agreed that she should creep into the shrine and steal the money box with her son strapped to her back with cloth. She travelled in the night to the haunted site and found the money box where it should be. Taking the box, she made her way back but heard a voice calling to her; in fear she began to run back to the safety of her friends, but when she arrived and turned around, her friends saw that the head of her infant son had been torn off or eaten and that blood covered her back.

King of Thieves

Ogata Shuma, also known as Jiraiya, was a prince whose father had died, leaving him without position. Joining a band of thieves, he soon became their leader-king and a nasty figure who involved himself in dark deeds. One night, taking refuge from a snowstorm, he stayed with an old woman in a hut during the blizzard. As the storm rattled the doors and windows, he drew his sword with the aim of killing her; however, his sword broke and the 'helpless' woman took the form a man who introduced himself as Dojin Senso, a toad spirit and magician. The disgraced prince entered into his service and learnt all he could of toad magic.

Later on he found himself an enemy called Orochimaru, an adept of snake magic who took the form of a giant snake. Orochimaru snuck into the prince's room and dripped venom on his head while he slept in a temple. The abbot of the temple immediately flew to India on the back of a winged *Tengu* to get the antidote; he arrived back at the temple just in time to save Jiraiya's life.

The Toad Robber

There was also a robber named Tokube who is said to have lived among frogs; he lived from 1619 to 1685.

Tsuneyori – The Snake Wrestler

Tsuneyori was a strongman and wrestler who was considered the strongest of men. One day he fell asleep at the base of a tree, and during his slumber a giant snake coiled itself around his legs. The body of the snake went through a river and its head came out on the opposite bank. The strongman awoke to the snake dragging him away, but after an epic struggle he took control of the snake and killed it with his bare hands. Unperturbed by the incident, he had men tie rope to his feet and pull on it so he could gauge how many men matched the strength of the snake; the final count was sixty men.

Another giant snake is Uwabami, which is a snake said to be so big it can swallow a mounted rider in one go.

The Demon Robber

Raiko (also known as Minamoto no Yorimitsu) had four great retainers: Watanabe no Tsuna, Urabe no Suekata, Usui Sadamitsu and Sakata no Kintoki. Together these men quested to kill demons and goblins, but one particularly interesting tale is that of Shutendoji. This scourge of the samurai was originally wealthy, but his father was killed and he was left destitute. Forced to join a band of thieves, he became a terror to the samurai. His group created a stronghold and also became demons with supernatural powers. The samurai of the land could not get rid of him, so Raiko stepped forward with his four retainers. He knew he could not storm the keep, so he decided on subterfuge instead. The troop dressed themselves as priests and carried their armour in travelling boxes, planning to enter the castle in this disguise. On the way they met with an old man – who was actually the spirit of the trio of Shinto gods known as Sumiyoshi – and he gave them a powerful potion and also a golden magical cap. They continued to travel on their quest and eventually came across a river, and here they found a woman weeping over the remains of her dead relative, killed by the bandits. Inspired, they moved on to the castle of thieves and begged shelter in their disguise as priests. They were welcomed in mock formality and they were ridiculed under a thin veil of politeness. Once admitted they saw hordes of female slaves and were fed a feast of human flesh, which they declared to love so as not to raise suspicion (making them all cannibals). In return for such a rich dish, Raiko told the leader that they had a magical drink that when mixed with ale would aid him greatly and give him power. The leader of the demons fell for the ploy and drank it down, at which point he fell asleep and took on his true devil form. Later, when all was quiet, the samurai 'priests' donned their armour and explained to the female slaves their plan. At this point, the old man – the spirit of Sumiyoshi who had given them the potion and the golden cap – appeared to aid them, this time giving Raiko a silk cord to bind the devil with. Raiko bound and decapitated the creature, but instead of dying the head flew around gnashing and biting everything. It looked at Raiko and went for him, clasping its demonic jaws on the hero, who was saved from death by the magical golden cap he was wearing on top of his helmet. The head was eventually killed and the body chopped up into sections, and all the demons that were his band of thieves were killed and all the slaves were freed.

The Fight at Rashomon Gate

Watanabe, one of the samurai in the above tale and a retainer to Raiko, continues at a later date with his friend, Hojo. They had asked Raiko if there were any demons left in all of Japan, and were told that there was a demon in Kyoto at the Rashomon gate. Watanabe set himself up for a night of demon slaying and nailed his intention to the door of the gate. At two in the morning he felt a tug at his helmet as the demon pulled him from above. Out flashed Watanabe's katana, and the vanquished demon's arm fell to the ground. Reminiscent of the story of Beowulf, Watanabe kept the arm in a box as a trophy. He keeps this arm as proof of his deeds but only shows it to very few people. One day a woman asks to see the arm, but this is no normal woman – it is his childhood nurse come to pay him a visit. After chatting he agrees to show her the arm, and as he lifts the box to display it she transforms into a devil in front of him, horns erupting from her head. The false childhood nurse grows into a full female *hanya* demon and steals the arm from him.

The Woman and Child

Urabe no Suekata, who was also among Raiko's retainers, was walking at night when a ghostly woman came from nowhere and gave him a baby to hold, at which point she vanished and he was left with the child.

Aunt's Wine

There once lived a boy who always wanted wine. His aunt would stop him from drinking as often as she could, so to get his hands on the drink he donned a demonic mask. Jumping out at her in his demon disguise, he demanded a drink. Frightened, she starts to pour this devil some wine, and after a few draughts the devil starts to talk and talk and the women realises that it is her nephew, whom she promptly beats.

The Loyal Three

There was once a samurai who was exiled from his land. On the evening before he departed, three friends came to attend his farewell dinner. The first gave him a lock of hair so he would remember him, the second cut off his nose and gave it to him as a keepsake, but the third committed ritual suicide there and then to prove his friendship.

The Skull Tree

Emperor Shirakawa Tenno suffered from headaches constantly. To find a solution to the pain he visited an Indian mystic and healer, who informed him that his headaches were coming because the skull which was his from a previous existence had floated down a river and snagged on a willow branch, which, having grown into maturity and carried the skull upwards, was now trapping the skull in its branches, held aloft under pressure. This same skull tree is connected to the legend of the famous archer Heitaro, who had married a tree sprite and whose own tree was the very one holding the skull. The tree-wife died when her tree was cut down, and when loggers tried to haul the tree past the archer's house, the trunk refused to move and could not be dragged away by any amount of force – that is until the son of the tree sprite and the archer, a young boy then, came out of the house and moved the great trunk alone. This story bears similarity to that of the samurai and the tree-wife (page 156).

The Smoking Tree

A samurai named Kodama Kuranojo was the commander of the Mori clan fleet during the sixteenth century. During a campaign, he anchored his ships and made a camp on Takasago beach. He ordered his men to cut down a tree, but for unknown reasons they did not want to do it. He confirmed his orders and forced his men to obey him; upon the first stroke of an axe into the tree it issued forth supernatural smoke, at which point he rescinded his orders.

The Tree on the Moon

This Chinese legend, which is popular in Japan, is about a Katsura tree (*Cercidiphyllum*) which is growing on the moon. Its leaves turn blood-red and if eaten turn you invisible. This legend even made its way into the world of the ninja, where the skill of tending to the trees on the moon is actually equated with planting a spy agent in enemy territory. The skill can be found in *The Book of Ninja*.

The Reading Wood Cutter

Shubaishin is a wood cutter who loves to read while walking. His wife, eager for promotion, leaves him because of his lowly status, but because of his self-education he is made governor, at which point the wife has a 'change of heart' and tries to reunite with him, to no avail. The wife and the lover she left him for end in dire straits and are so poor they have to beg forgiveness, but in the end they commit suicide.

The Lost Couple

Once there was a young and loving couple. Along comes a rich merchant (let's pretend he is old and evil) who wants to marry the young girl. Her parents say yes to the marriage, and so the young lovers are distraught. They soon decide to enter into a suicide pact. They embrace, and the man kills the woman before cutting his own throat. However, to his misery someone finds him and sends for a surgeon, who saves his life. After some time the man recovers and goes on trial for murder. He is given a light sentence as the Japanese understand the suicide pact as an act of honour, but when he gets out of prison he fails to finish the job and kill himself. After this he lives seven years in agony, and people of the area say that it was the ghost of his dead lover, upset that he did not follow on after her, who is causing his suffering.

The Maiden and Her Lovers by Evelyn Paul.

The Maiden of Unai

There was once a beautiful samurai girl who had attracted the attention of two men, each of whom wanted her hand in marriage. Both of them were equal in looks, gifts and manner. This was quite a dilemma, and the fair maiden was tormented by her inability to choose. After much deliberation it was said that a contest should be held in which the two suitors would shoot at a bird. They both shot at the same time and both hit the bird. The maiden, beyond distress, throws herself into the river but the two samurai grab her – at the same time – and all three fall in and drown. The three were buried, one samurai each side of the lover, and the site is known as the Maiden's Grave.

The Lover's Swim

In Izu there was a fisherman's daughter who was a great swimmer and used to swim at night several miles to her lover, who was across the water. One night, the light that the male lover would shine for her as a guide was left unattended. It went out, and she lost her way in the dark and drowned. The next day her body washed ashore. Hearn talks of a Japanese folk saying: 'The sea has a soul and can hear you. If you express your fear, the sea will know of it and rise against you.'

Bird Daughters

There was once a man called Okada who was a *ronin* who loved to hunt. Often he would go into the wild with muskets loaded to shoot birds. His two daughters hated this sport and pleaded with him to stop, but he continued his bloodthirsty hobby. So, one moonlit evening, they dressed as two white storks and went to his hunting ground. From afar he thought them birds and took aim, shooting and killing both. Upon inspection, to his horror he discovered that he had killed his own children. After this he shaved his head and became a monk and never killed again.

The Murdering Father

There was once a peasant who was very poor. His wife bore him six children, but each time one was born he threw it into the river and told people that it had died in childbirth. Later in his life he became better off and enjoyed a few luxuries. His wife gave birth to the seventh child, and this time he kept it. Loving the child very much, one night he took it into the garden to show it the moon. The infant took on the voice of a grown man and said, 'It looks the same as it did when you threw me in the river all those times.' The man, understanding the enormity of his crimes, became a priest.

The Family of Sparrows

An old man had a pet sparrow. When he was out one day, his evil neighbour saw it eating from her garden and so captured it and cut out its tongue. The old man, noticing his sparrow gone, searched the woods and came upon a small house, where his pet sparrow had returned to its family. The old man is taken in and given shelter and food. When leaving, the sparrow family offer him one of two boxes to take home. The old man, being old, said he would take the smaller one as it would be less of a burden. Returning home, the old man opened the package with his wife to find fine cloth and treasure inside. The evil neighbour, seeing this, ran into the forest to the same house and demanded a box. Given the same choice, she left with the larger box; when she opened it, demons and goblins sprung out to torment her.

The Tortoise and the Magic Box

Urashima Taro was fishing one day when he caught a tortoise, but instead of keeping and eating it he spared its life. A short while later, a woman was shipwrecked and he found himself saving another life from the sea. However, this was in fact the same tortoise in the guise of a woman, and she was the daughter to the Dragon King of the Sea. In reward, she took him to live in her domain. After three years he started to become homesick, wanting to return to his family. In the end she let him return, and gifted him a magical box. On his return, however, much time had passed and all his family were dead; he found only a grave to mark their existence. In desperation he opened the box; it contained his youth. With this he aged and died instantly. Three hundred years had passed in the three that he had been gone.

Susa-no-o and the Magic Comb

Once a god called Susa-no-o passed a weeping couple. On being asked what was the matter, the couple said that their daughter, Kushinada-hime, was their eighth daughter and was the only one left as the other seven were sent to a sea serpent to be sacrificed. The serpent had eight heads, and so their final daughter was to be the eighth sacrifice. Susa-no-o said he would save her in return for her hand in marriage. The bargain struck, the god turned Kushinada-hime into a wooden comb and put her in his hair. He took eight jugs of *sake* and gave them to the serpent, which became drunk. Then, when he felt the time was right, he killed the beast, returned Kushinada-hime to her human form and married her.

It is of interest that in the early 1700s this legend was recorded by a ninja of the land of Iga. He states that this is origin of the arts of the ninja, because the god transformed the comb as a ninja would transform and disguise himself, making it the first time the arts of deception were used in Japan – according to ninja lore. The full story can be read in *Iga and Koka Ninja Skills*.

Prince Yamato and the Mountain Serpent

Prince Yamato is a famous figure and achieved many things, but one of his darker deeds is as follows. In the land of Omi, there was a great wailing as a mountain serpent had caused the people much pain. Climbing the mountain, Yamato found the creature and strangled it with his bare hands. When it died, the sky darkened and rain fell in sheets. He descended the mountain when the weather cleared, but found that he had pains in his feet – he had been stung with venom. He was taken to a spring where the sun goddess cured him.

Tokoyo and the Sea Serpent

There was once a samurai who was banished to the island of Oki and left behind a daughter. The daughter was so distraught that she took passage near to the islands and tried to reunite with her father. Fishermen asked her not to go and to leave well alone, but on a moon-filled night she took a light craft and landed on Oki alone. She climbed up the rocks only to find a priest was about to push a girl, dressed in white, into the waters because if a maiden was not sacrificed then the seas would rage. The daughter offered to stand in for the poor girl and changed clothes with her. She jumped into the sea, swam down to the bottom and found the cave of a sea serpent. Drawing a dagger from her mouth, she killed it. She returned to the surface, was reunited with her father and they returned home.

Fujiwara and the Legends of Kamatari

Fujiwara is one of the founding families in Japanese history, and many samurai lines claim descent from the Fujiwara clan. Kamatari is said to be the founder of the Fujiwara line, and he supposedly gave his daughter's hand in marriage to the emperor of China. When in China, his daughter found a most marvellous jewel and put it on a ship home to her father. Demons, hearing of this great jewel, attacked the ship but could not get the prize from it. After a short while, there came a log on the water; clinging to it was a maiden who was beautiful and fair. After being rescued and having enchanted the crew she was shown the jewel, at which point she snatched it and dived into the ocean, taking it to the Dragon King of the Sea. Later, the privileged Kamatari left his position and wealth behind and took to the mountains. Here he married a common woman and was happy. However, one day he told his wife of his previous status and of his problem with the jewel and the Dragon King. Thinking she could never live knowing she was so low and he so high, his wife ran to the sea and swam to the palace of the Dragon King, where she stole back the jewel. All manner of creatures followed her, but she took a knife and stabbed herself in the chest. As the blood spilled from her, it formed a veil between her and the monsters. Kamatari, looking for his wife on the sea, finds her and pulls her onto his boat, where she gives him the jewel and dies.

The Monster of Lake Biwa

There was a man named Hidesato who was walking near Lake Biwa when he came upon a mighty dragon. Completely unfazed, he walked over the dragon as a bridge and got to the opposite bank. When he had crossed, he looked back and the dragon bridge was gone; instead a man with a dragon crown stood next to him. The man said he was the Dragon King of Lake

Biwa. He said that he had been looking for a brave man and that Hidesato was the first to not flee upon seeing him. He then went on to explain that he was being attacked by the giant centipede of Mt Mikami and asked Hidesato for help. Venturing to kingdom in Lake Biwa, Hidesato saw such great wonders as dancing fish and fish on 'harps' (long before Disney thought of such things), but during a feast there was a disruption and from Mt Mikami came a centipede the size of the mountain itself, with balls of fire for eyes and legs like a line of glowing lanterns. Hidesato took up his bow and loosed a great arrow, but it glanced off the armour of his enemy's head; he sent another arrow forth, but again it bounced off. Taking his final arrow in hand, he licked the point – human saliva is poisonous to centipedes – and took careful aim and fired. This time the shaft hit hard, and from the dark mountain the eyes of fire dimed and a storm brewed; the evil creature died, but gave birth to a tempest. The following morning the people saw the mighty foe dead in the water and the Dragon King of Lake Biwa held another royal feast and gave Hidesato gifts: a bag of rice, a roll of silk, some bells and a cooking pot. But these were no ordinary gifts; the cooking pot did not need fire, the roll of silk never ended, the bells were magical and the bag of rice was forever full. After this the hero became famous and was known as the Lord of the Bag of Rice.

The Spirit of the Sword

One night a ship anchored off Fundo Cape and the crew fell asleep on the deck. The captain heard a tremendous rumble and a maiden clad in white came up through the water and said she wished to return to the land. The next day, the captain asked the local people of this and they said it was the spirit of a maiden who had drowned and been lost in the waters. As a result of the pollution caused by a human corpse in the water, the god of the sea had taken away all the fish in the bay. A fellow called Sankichi was asked to dive and find the bones of the woman but could find none. Instead, he found a shining sword on the sea floor which was not affected by the waters and had remained clean. Bringing this up and recovering from almost drowning, he gave his story and the sword was put in a shrine; the fish then came back to the bay.

The Mother-Ghost

In Matsue there was a shopkeeper who was visited each night by a pale woman in white who always bought one *rin*'s worth of nourishment. The shopkeeper became curious and followed her, but stopped as she entered the cemetery. The next night he had friends join him and investigate. Again the woman came to buy the food and left; this time they followed her to a tomb, and found she walked through the wall. They opened the tomb because they heard the laughing of a child. When they went in they saw the ghost woman and a human child taking in the nourishment that the woman had paid for. It turns out that the woman was buried prematurely and had given birth in the tomb. She came out as a ghost each night to keep her child alive.

The Necromancer

Once there lived a necromancer called Saji who was very skilled; he could even produce fish from a bowl of clear water (presumably he could also speak with the dead). His master, who once loved him, became tired and wanted rid of him and his magic. One of the master's court aides captured him and tried to cut him down, but his sword would not bite. He tried to burn him, but Saji leapt and flew out of the flames to safety and mingled with a herd of goats, changing into one of them. The court aide had all the goats decapitated, but missed the necromancer. Saji, feeling sorry for the goats but in a terrible rush, magically put all the heads back on the goats but unfortunately in the wrong order and thus the herd was a living mismatch of heads on the wrong bodies.

Eggs and Mionoseki

The god of the place called Mionoseki hates eggs and chickens, and therefore eggs and chickens of any kind are banned from the temple and surrounding area. The god controls the seas and storms, and any sailor who dares bring fowl near the temple will be cursed. In fact, it is said that if you had an egg for breakfast then you must wait for the following day to visit the temple, lest the god punish you.

The Witch Lover

The lord of the island of Kyushu had an enemy in a witch named Shiriranui, who used her magic to make him fall in love with a woman called Mikuni Kojoro. The witch killed Kojoro and replaced her with a doppelganger who remained the concubine of the lord. This 'Kojoro' became powerful and in the end ruined and killed the lord, making it a victory for the witch.

Shosei and the Eyes of Lightning

This gentleman, if he opened his eyes, would emit bolts of lightning and claps of thunder, destroying all around him. To stop the destruction, he closed his eyes for twenty years; he was helped in this state by twenty aides. One day one of his followers persuaded him to open his eyes, just a little, to see what would happen. He did so, and everyone was knocked out in a flash of light and a roar of sound.

The Hunger of the Thunder God

For some unknown reason, the god of thunder in Japan loves to eat navels. One ancient gentleman decided he wanted to kill the god of thunder, so in true 'hero' style he murdered a woman and stole her navel, attaching it to a kite to lure down the god of thunder so that he could kill him. The thunder god saw this and went for the bait (not such a clever god). He took the navel and began to chew it; however, the 'murdered' woman had actually lived through the attempted murder. She got her navel back in the end and the man got to fight the thunder god – overall, this legend is one of Japan's strangest.

Thunder God to the Rescue

A man was once attacked by robbers in the woods and in his flight he called on the god of thunder to save him. The god and devils answered his prayers and came to his rescue. The robbers tried again, but this time the man was waiting for them with nets and traps and a little help from the gods.

The Ancient Warrior

Takenouchi no Sukune is said to have lived in the early part of the first millennium and was thought to have reached the age of 280, although other accounts have him at 360 years old. Either way, he was meant to have been of an age that no human can reach today.

The Zombie Land of Mukeikoku

In this mythical land live people who dwell in holes in the ground (no, not Hobbits) and have no stomachs (definitely not Hobbits) but eat earth as a steady diet. When they die they are placed in the ground, where they are reborn.

The Samurai Boy and His Father's Head

Once a lord called a young samurai boy to his quarters and placed a decapitated head in front of him. The lord asked the boy whether or not it was the head of his father. The boy realised that a situation must have arisen where an imposter had been used so his father could flee. The boy, seeing that the head was actually not that of his father, saluted it in the manner that would be deemed appropriate if it had been his father and there and then he committed suicide on the spot; the lord was thus assured that the head was his father's. In truth, the father escaped capture and the boy became a legend.

The Cave of the Spider

Earlier we heard about the famed demon killer Raiko and his archery expertise. Raiko had other adventures, and in this episode he was travelling with his friend Watanabe no Tsuna. One day they saw a giant skull coming in and out of the clouds, blood-red and with a beaming halo. They moved into action and followed the giant red skull until they came to a rocky area, and there they saw Yama-uba, a mountain hag. She sat at a cave entrance, her breasts hanging down to the floor, with an ivory wand in one hand. She used the end of the wand to open her mouth and her extremely heavy eyelids. Raiko argued with her, demanding that she show him the entrance to any demon's hiding place, but she refused; ignoring her, the two of them searched and found a cave entrance. The cave was inhabited by a troop of female ghosts with a female leader, an enchantress who brought the men under a spell and wrapped them in green cobwebs. Waking from the spell he cut left and right, slashing out with his sword. Getting free, he saw in the darkness of the cave a milky white glow trailing into the black – a thread of luminescence. Presuming this to be her blood trail, they followed it deeper and deeper into the cave. At last they came out into a chamber, but found themselves confronted by a huge spider of gigantic size (this is just *Lord of the Rings* now!) where they did battle. It is said that each leg was the size of a bargepole, and each had spines like iron swords. Fighting with the titanic arachnid, Raiko's sword breaks as he wounds the spider. However, undeterred, he calls on Shoki, the demon-killer god, to help him; taking a massive swing with his sword, he decapitates the spider-demon in one go. Standing over the corpse, they split open the belly of the creature and some 1,919 warrior's skulls come out; to their surprise, so do a hundred 3-foot spiders. The two set about killing them all, ending the tale of the spider-demon.

Other episodes including spiders have men casting iron nets at the entrances to spider caves and then smoking out the cave system with giant fires and thick smoke.

The Mean Old Man

An old man was so mean with his money that he kept all for himself, but later in life he found that he was ill. On the tenth night of his illness, a monk came to his side and said that if he let go of his huge money belt and gave his wealth to others his illness would abate. The old man slashed out with his dagger and the lights went out. His servants came in and found a clawed, hairy hand on the floor and followed the blood trail into the garden to a miniature hill where there was a spider's hole and a spider bleeding nearby. The spider was the goddess Inari. It had been her that had advised the old man.

Mountain Hag and Mountain Man

There are various stories of hags in the mountains, and normally the crone archetype is used. The male version is described as large in appearance, hairy like a monkey and extremely strong. He will come into villages and take food from stores and such.

The Head-Washing Well

The legend of the forty-seven *ronin* is one that the whole world knows; the story of these loyal samurai and their vengeance upon the enemy of their lord has been seen in film and on the stage. However, many people are unaware that you can actually go and see the graves of the warriors, and also the well in which they washed their enemy's head before they presented it to the grave of their master. It is at Sanjakuji temple in Tokyo, and visitors are more than welcome.

A view of the temple in 1900.

An old woodblock print of the well where the head was washed.

Jizo and the Ronin's Wife

Jizo is a saint and protector of children. One day, the wife of a *ronin* made a small cloth cap to keep the statue of Jizo warm; she said that she was sorry that she could not afford to buy cloth to make clothes to cover him in full. Later on the wife died, but her body remained fresh for three days, which stopped her being cremated as people thought it strange. In these three days she was in the kingdom of Hell and the Regent of Hell was punishing her. He said that she had killed many silkworms in her lifetime during her work and therefore she was to be boiled in molten metal for all eternity. However, just as she was getting into the pot, Jizo thundered through Hell to her rescue and told the Regent of Hell that he owed her a debt of gratitude and so the master of Hell let her go back to her body. The wife talks with Jizo and asks if it is a crime to use silkworms so that they die, to which he answers yes, most certainly – but then, reaching over, he whispers in her ear with a smile, 'But all priests wear silk!'

The Fall of the Ronin

Once there was a youthful samurai called Gompachi who was skilled at swordplay, and one day his dog tangled with another samurai's dog. The two samurai, being young, set to a duel, which Gompachi won. Having murdered his opponent, he fled and became a *ronin* and made for the city of Edo. Poor but armed with a good sword, he stopped at an inn. Unbeknown to him, the inn was a den of thieves. Late in the night, when he was asleep, the door opened up and a young maiden entered. She woke him and said that he was in danger and that the keepers were actually a band of thieves and that she had been kidnapped from her house in Mikawa. Promising to take her with him, Gompachi pretended to be asleep when the robbers came in; before they knew it, he had cut one down and then another and at last found his way to freedom, and he and the maiden made their way to Mikawa and to her parents. Overjoyed to be reunited with their daughter, the parents tried to make the young *ronin* marry her. He said that he must leave as he was on his way to Edo to make his name, but that he would return. Understanding his intentions, the parents let him leave with the generous gift of 200 ounces of silver. On the road to Edo he was accosted by some bandits and fought off two of the six; they started to get the upper hand, but just then a famous warden of the district came to his aid and saved him from the robbers. The warden took him into his house and put a roof over his head and all was well. However, soon the *ronin* started to fall into ill repute, frequenting brothels and malicious places. Months went by and he did not find employment and more and more of his money was spent on prostitutes. One day he heard of a new and beautiful prostitute who was said to be the most beautiful woman in Edo, and so he paid to see her. Alas! It was his promised bride, and she had entered into the sex slave industry voluntarily. Her parents had fallen on hard times and had become bankrupt so as a remedy for the situation she had sold herself to help them out, but it did not help as they sank into more debt and in the end died of grief. The once wealthy daughter was thus stuck as a lady of the night. More and more the *ronin* visited her, and more of his money was lost until he had none. Without cash, and now slung out of the warden's house, he was set in a life of murder and robbery, and one by one his victims mounted up, but each time that he killed he could afford to see the love that he should have been happy with at the start. Eventually his killings became so much that spies were set on his case (interestingly, this was the job for a ninja in these days) and they tracked him down, captured him and dragged him to an execution ground to be killed as you would kill a dog: he was bound and beheaded. The maiden – a maiden no longer – was devastated by his death. She learnt that the kind warden had buried her love and given him a grave, so she hatched a plan to flee the brothel. One night she crept out of the house, ran to his grave and stabbed herself until she died, and there on her lover's grave she lay.

The Samurai and the Englishman

Hearn tells the story of an unnamed Englishman from the days of empire (meaning he was something of an elitist) who, while in Japan, hired a samurai to teach him Japanese. The samurai, seeing his employer as a 'lord', would bow to him and bring gifts, which led the Englishman to see him as a servant and not an employee, and a forced relationship grew. One day an argument ensued, and the Englishman struck the samurai, who drew his sword. However, before he attacked, he reflected and then replaced it in its scabbard and left. That night the samurai committed suicide by ritual disembowelment because he could not strike a man with whom he had a lord–retainer relationship, and also the Englishman had loaned him money in a time of need. However, the Englishman, being English, did not understand the offence he had caused, and presumably thought all would be reconciled. With the samurai dead, he never got his chance – a true cultural misunderstanding.

Monkey on the Emperor's Roof

For many nights there was a cloud of thunder on the roof of the emperor's palace, and no one could understand what it was until it changed into a monster-monkey with terrible claws and began crying at the moon. Night after night it came, so Yorimasa, a famed archer-poet, shot the beast down to the ground. This creature was a *nuye*. It had the head of a monkey, the claws of a tiger, the back of a badger and the tail of a snake. As it lay wounded, Hayata Tadazumi killed it and that was the end of the beast.

Yorimasa and the Monster-monkey Cloud by Evelyn Paul.

Fox-witch

Remembering that the fox is a creature of supreme supernatural power, we come to the tale of Tamamo no Maye, who was a concubine to the emperor but also a fox-witch. There was a great illness over the land, and the people were confused as to why. One of the priests, suspecting Tamamo of witchcraft, erected an altar and asked everyone to pray before it; to the priest's bemusement, she avoided giving supplication and prayer. At last she was directly summoned to pray, and as she approached the holy altar she began to transform in to a white fox with nine tails (making her over 1,000 years old), at which point she flew away into the sky.

Hoichi the Earless

There was once a blind musician who played at night outside the Akamagaseki memorial, which was a tribute to the Taira clan, who fell in the Genpei War. As the blind musician was an excellent player and told of the war in his songs, a ghost of the dead Taira clan came out to hear him. The ghost led him by the hand to a location inside the cemetery and asked the blind man to play for the crowd of 'samurai'. Night after night he returned, playing for the dead samurai of old – a fact he did not know as he was blind and bewitched. The temple where he was staying sent out men to drag him back by force and awaken him from this bewitchment. So frightened was he by his haunted audience that the next day he asked the priest for help. The priest said that he was called away on business but that he would have his apprentice write many holy sutras on him so that the dead could not see him. Also, he warned him not to say a word even when the ghosts surrounded him and spoke to him. That day, the apprentice wrote the sutras all over Hoichi's body. As night fell the ghosts returned and tried to speak with Hoichi, but found that all they could see was a *biwa* (lute) playing itself and two ears floating in the air. The ghosts, not getting an answer from the musician, tore the ears away and took them with them. The priest returned the next day and apologised, saying that the apprentice had not written the holy words upon his ears – a beginner's mistake.

Fire in Legend

Japan has a few legends about fire, such as ghost-fire, demon-fire, fox-flame, flash-pillars, badger-blaze, dragon-torch and the lamp of Buddha, in addition to fire-wheels (messengers from hell), sea-fires and flames that erupt from cemeteries.

In Settsu there is said to be a globe of fire that hovers over a tree from March to June with a face in the flames. This has its origins in the tale of a sick woman and her governor husband, who had an exorcist named Nikobo perform rites of exorcism to rid her of evil. When Nikobo succeeded, the governor was jealous of his success (and power over his wife?) and had him executed. From that point on, the face of the exorcist was seen in the flames and the fear of this eventually killed the governor.

Another tale of fire comes from Kadachi Hills, where fire is said to appear over a lake and when the flames rise they take the form of two wrestlers engaged in combat. Be warned, if you try to interfere with their fighting you will be thrown a great distance.

Also, it was bad luck to throw some things onto a fire. Two such things were persimmon seeds and the *Lycoris* plant – it was thought that a fire would take revenge by burning down your house. The warning about the *Lycoris* plant may be due to the appearance of its flower, which is reminiscent of fire.

The Concubine and the Lord's Wife

Once there was a lord whose wife had been ill for three whole years, and none of the treatments she had received, nor the prayers of monks nor the fasting of her husband, helped her to recover. When death was inevitable, her husband went to her side and said that after she had died he would spend gold securing prayers said on her behalf to encourage a better birth in the next life. To this the wife said that all she required was the brief company of his favourite concubine, Lady Yukiko, so that she may discuss with

Yukiko her duties as she was to become the lord's wife after she had passed. Lady Yukiko was brought to her bedside and spoke to the dying wife, who asked her to take her on her back and carry her to the garden to see the blooming of the 'double-flowered cherry blossom tree'. Yukiko bent down to take the wife on her back, but as she did so the dying wife leapt up with superhuman force, pushing her hands through the top of Yukiko's robes and grabbing her breasts, crying out triumphantly. With this the wife died, and they both fell forward. However, as people tried to remove the corpse of the wife from Yukiko, they found that the hands had stuck fast to her breasts and that the skin of both the breasts and the hands had merged to form one mass. Surgeons could not understand how this had happened, and in the end a Dutch surgeon was summoned. He said that it was unlike anything he had seen and he recommended cutting the corpse at the wrists at least to take the body away; as this was done, the hands shrivelled and turned black. This was not the end, as at the hour of the Ox each night the hands came to life, squeezing the breasts hard and causing pain, and they did so for two hours until it was the hour of the Tiger, at which point they stopped. Lady Yukiko became a nun and prayed to appease the spirit of the wife, wandering the country. She was last seen in 1846.

Holy Pictures

There was once a holy man who was poor beyond measure and had not the means to feed himself. To remedy his hunger he decided to paint images to sell along the road. The problem was that he was so holy that what he painted came to life, and not only that – the paintings even issued thunder and lightning, making them a hard sell.

The Dead Wife's Revenge

There was once a samurai who disliked his wife but loved his mistress, O-sode. He decided to poison his wife, and after the deed was done her ghost wished for revenge. Haunting the samurai without end, the tormented spirit drove the samurai to kill everyone around him until there was only O-sode left, whom he also killed, leaving the samurai alone.

The Painter and the Girl

Once there was a great student painter called Sawara who lived with a master to learn his art. Kimi, the daughter of the master, fell in love with him and they were to be married. Before he could marry her, though, Sawara had to go to another master of greater renown and further his career. Two years went by and Kimi had no word from him; letters were sent and he was sought out, but to no avail. In fact the apprentice Sawara had married another, but happened to come upon Kimi one day; she was unmarried and still waiting. On discovering he was married, she rushed into the sea hut and killed herself with a knife. Sawara followed in after her, but on seeing her dead form he simply drew a picture of her and painted it in full to keep her memory alive. Unfortunately, what happened was too true to his wishes. Each night the painting came to life and haunted his house, so much so that he had to give the painting to a temple and pray that the soul of Kimi would move on.

Unkei the Artist to the Regent of Hell

The artist Unkei was met after his death by Yemma, the Regent of Hell. The regent loved Unkei's work so much that he brought him back to life and commanded him to return to earth and create a statue in his image. The statue is said to be at Ennoji temple in Kamakura.

Follow the Bell

Similar to the above, one Ono no Kimi was also told that he must return to earth by the Regent of Hell, but he said he did not know the way nor could he retrace his footsteps. The Regent of Hell told him to listen and follow the pealing of the Engakuji temple bell, and that way he would find himself back in the world of humans.

Hell Is Full

Another person to escape from Hell was Tokudo Shonin, who died and ended up in front of Yemma. The regent told him that Hell was full because people were not visiting the thirty-three holy sites which were dedicated to Kwannon. He was sent back to earth for three days to tell people the news and prevent Hell from overflowing with souls.

Buddha and His Trip to Hell

One legend says that Nanda was a student of the Buddha but was captivated by the beauty of women. To help his disciple, Buddha took him to Hell (after he had taken him on a trip to Heaven) and showed a vat of molten metal which was coming to the boil but had no occupant; he told Nanda it was his. A demon who was stood next to the boiling substance said that this cauldron was waiting for a man named Nanda who would waste his chance at enlightenment and squander his days on beautiful women – at this point he got the idea.

Japanese Voodoo

(Well, not quite voodoo.) There is a tale of a young man who made wooden figures of his dead parents. One day he returned home to find that the previously happy-looking figures now bore sad expressions. His wife saw this and decided to test them; she got a pin and pricked the dolls. Blood oozed out.

Japanese Dolls

Japanese dolls are famous the world over, but what is not known is that while Japanese belief held that a new doll is merely a doll, if the same doll is played with for generations by children of the same family then the doll acquires a soul and is a living thing. It is even said that one doll got up and ran to safety when its house was on fire. This is similar to the aforementioned idea of *tsukumogami*, living objects.

The Demon Queller

In ancient China there lived a man called Shoki who studied hard; however, he failed his exams and did not gain the qualifications he desired. In dire straits, he killed himself. When the Chinese emperor found out about this he buried him with honour out of respect for his dedication. In death, Shoki committed himself to rid the land of China of all demons. He is depicted killing or beating demons, but at times in the illustrations demons are hidden to comic effect, keeping out of his way. Sometimes he is shown with pain on his face from having Moxa treatment, wherein a burning herb is placed on the skin. Despite Chinese origins, the figure of Shoki was very popular in Japan.

The Ghost of Sakura Castle

At the time of this legend, the land was ruled with an iron fist by Tokugawa Iemitsu. The lord of Soma, Kotsuke, ruled Sakura Castle; he was cruel and sadistic and decided to tax the people heavily, taking them to the limit. The people joined together and made an appeal to Edo, the capital, but the appeal failed, at which the people marched towards Sakura Castle and the cruel lord. The leader of this peaceful rebellion was a man named Sogoro, and yet again they could not sway the lord's mind. Desperate, they decided to travel again to Edo, hoping to get the shogun's help, and this time eleven people from the village made their way along the highways of Japan to the capital, full of hope. Yet again their hopes were dashed, but this time seven of the party of eleven remained in the capital to carry on their crusade of justice. They forged a plan where they would hide under a bridge and wait for the shogun to come past so that that they could drop a petition into his lap. When he passed by, Sogoro threw the document into his litter but was immediately arrested and thrown into jail. For this grave insult to the person of the shogun, both Sogoro and his wife were sentenced to be crucified. But this was not enough; their three sons, aged seven, ten and thirteen, would be beheaded while they hung on the cross. The other six people involved in the incident were to be banished, but they pleaded with the authorities and asked to die in place of the wife and children – their offer was refused. In 1646 the sentence was carried out and the crucified parents watched their children beheaded as they hung. Sogoro, on his cross, vowed to haunt Kotsuke's family. He shouted that when he died his lifeless head would turn towards the castle and his spirit would take vengeance. From that time onwards, Kotsuke's room was filled with ghosts and evil, so much so that it drove the lord's wife insane and she died. The lord, repentant, erected a memorial stone but in the end went mad and killed people in terror. This was the sad case of Sakura Castle.

O-tei – The Reincarnated Wife

In Echizen there was a man called Nagao Chosei who was to be married to his love, O-tei, but O-tei became ill and was near death. Before she died, she said to Nagao that it was their fate to meet for seven lives and that he would meet and marry her again in this lifetime if he would just wait for her. He promised that he would wait for his love, and she died in his arms. After the correct rites had been performed he created a death tablet for her and wrote out the promise they had made and put it on his altar. However, being samurai, he had a duty to marry and was forced into an arranged marriage. After many years his parents and wife and also his son died. One day he was visiting a spring town called Ikao, and, stopping at an inn, he was served by a young woman. His heart leapt as she was very reminiscent of O-tei, but to satisfy himself he asked her probing questions. In the ghostly voice of the spirit of O-tei she proclaimed his name and her former name and the promise they had. She spoke of their intended marriage and how she was back to fulfil the promise. The girl fell down unconscious and on waking could not recall the incident, and nor did she talk as the dead again, but they married and were reunited.

Ghost Poem

There is a poem on ghosts which is translated by Clara A. Walsh:

> It is an awesome thing
> to meet a-wandering,
> in the dark night,
> the dark and rainy night,
> a phantom greenish-grey,
> ghost of some Wight,
> poor Wight,
> wandering lonesomely
> through the black of night.

The Beautiful Nun

Once there was a beautiful woman of the court who was young and much admired. However, she wanted to become a nun. Visiting the temple, she asked the priest to take her into the order but the priest told her that she was young, powerful and had a full life before her and that her beauty was too much of an issue. He continued his refusal by telling her she would not fit in well as a nun because of her youth and her extreme good looks, but still she pleaded on. In the end, the priest left the room and waited for her to leave. However, she did not leave. Instead she put iron tongs in the fire of the brazier, and when red hot she held them to her face, burning her flesh and disfiguring her beauty. After this the priest accepted her into the order.

O-same and the Haunted Robe

Once a young woman was walking in town when she spied a most beautiful samurai in the gorgeous robes of his rank. At once she was in love. She did not have the opportunity to talk with him, and when home she thought of him all day. The woman decided on a plan. She would make purple robes with symbols like his own and wear them around town to draw his attention and win his heart. However, she never saw him again and spent nights crying over the robe, eventually falling ill and dying. The robe was then given to the temple as was custom, but the monk decided to sell the expensive item. The robes were bought by a young woman, but when she brought them home she was haunted by images of a beautiful samurai and soon died. Again the robe returned to the temple, but again it was sold and another girl died in pain; yet again it was returned and resold, and yet again it killed and was returned. This time the monk decided that it was a robe of ill will and ordered a fire to be lit in the temple area. When he threw the robe on the fire, the flames leapt up in the air and formed ideograms which had been used in a prayer – the very prayer O-same had used when she prayed for her samurai love. These flame-spirit letters reached the roof of the temple and it burst into flame, but woe, there is more – the fire spread all across Edo. This fire was in the 1650s and is remembered as the Great

Fire of the Long-sleeved Robe. The fire was real, but this is the legend.

The Gracious King and the Assassin

Yoji Chi served King Chihaku, but King Chihaku fell under the sword of his rival King Chojoshi. Chojoshi took the head of the fallen king and sawed through the top of the skull, having the skull lacquered to use as a drinking vessel. The servant Yoji Chi was outraged and wanted revenge for his fallen leader. During the first attempt to assassinate the king he was captured, but the king spared his life, knowing he was a loyal retainer on a sacred quest of vengeance. Next he dressed as a leper and waited under a bridge; again he was stopped, and again the king forgave him. Standing there in front of such a fine king, Yoji asked for the king's cloak so that he could symbolically hack it to 'death', thus achieving his goal of revenge. He killed himself when he was done, as his task was complete.

13

LEGENDS FROM TONO

The following short collection comprises legends and stories collected by the late Mr Yanagita, a devotee of folklore preservation who at the end of the nineteenth century and in the first half of the twentieth century collected folk tales from various areas. Given the period in which he worked, the tales are relatively modern. While this is just a selection, it includes some of the more grotesque stories collected from Tono in Iwate prefecture.

Choja's Daughter

One day a daughter of the Choja family was kidnapped, and after a while was presumed dead. Years later, a huntsman went hunting in a mountainous area that was seldom visited. It was in this area that he found a girl. He took aim – for some reason any story in the collection with a girl and a hunter has the hunter trying to shoot the unarmed girl – but she cried out, saying that he was in fact her uncle and that she had been kidnapped years ago. She had been forced to have babies with her kidnapper, but when they were delivered he ate them up, cannibalising his own offspring. Upon hearing this the hunter ran away in fear, and when he got back to the village he had forgotten the position and a rescue could not be attempted.

Mt Goyo

On Mount Goyo there lived a woman who had been kidnapped by a man with strange and piercing eyes. She gave him baby after baby, but he said they were not his and took them away; when she was freed she said that she believed he ate or killed them.

The Fall of the House of Choja

The house of Choja was a prominent family in the village, with a history that went back a long way. One day, the people of the house found some strange mushrooms that had never been seen before. Some of the members said they should not eat the mushrooms, but one family member said that they knew a way to nullify any poison – this was done by soaking them in water and mixing the water with a few grasses. They all agreed to try and cook them in this manner. After diner they all grew ill, and one by one they died – apart from a small girl who was playing outside and did not attend the dinner. People in the village came to the Choja residence and took goods, claiming they were owed money by the family; in the end only a bare shell of a house remained. Thus passed the house of Choja, an ancient family that fell in a single day.

Howling Wolf

One night the wolves were howling loudly, and a drunken man on his way home decided he would join the cacophony; to his dismay, the wolves came to join the howl around him. He fled into his house, but the wolves surrounded his house and howled all night long. In the morning he found that the wolves had gotten into his livestock and killed many of his animals, and from that day on the house was an unlucky one.

Tetsu and the Wolf

Tetsu means "iron" in Japanese and so the gentleman in this story is named "Iron" because he was as hard as metal. Tetsu was a large man and wrestled as a pass time, we should think of him as the village strongman. The village were being plagued by wolves so Tetsu, being the strongest went out to fight them, no weapons in hand. The Alpha backed away from him but the female came on. Tetsu wrapped his kimono jacket around his arm and forced his hand into the she-wolf's mouth, at the same time the she-wolf bit down. He called for aid but no one would move, so he reached down and forced his hand into the stomach of the she-wolf as the she-wolf gnawed at his upper arm. The wolf died there but Tetsu was carried back to the village where he died of his wounds, thus ends the story of Tetsu – the man of iron.

Kuma and the Bear

Kuma in Japanese means bear, and this gentleman was named so because of his fight with such an animal. One day, some friends were in the mountains when a bear attacked them, or at least threatened them. The man wrestled the bear and both fell down a steep hillside into a river; as the rest looked on, they saw that the bear had died but the man survived. Thus did he take on his new name.

Monkeys in Armour

This is the tale of a monkey that had somehow melted pine resin and mixed it with sand, covering his fur in the mixture. When dry, the mixture became hard like armour and even bullets could not stop him. It is interesting to know that pine resin, crushed bone and sand do indeed form a hard substance.

The *Kappa* in the Bucket

Kappa are strange sea creatures (as discussed earlier), and once in the area of Tono a *kappa* lost its way from the water and took refuge under a bucket. When the village people saw the bucket, they wondered why it was upside-down. As they tried to lift it, they saw the hand of a *kappa* and all wondered what to do. An agreement with the *kappa* was made and it arranged to leave the village alone if they let it go. It is said that the *kappa* still haunts a pond nearby.

The Sly Fox

One day a hunter was poised to shoot down a fox. He took aim at the creature, but it stopped dead in its tracks and looked at the hunter with an expression of indifference. When the hunter shot, nothing happened. Looking at his weapon, the hunter found that the barrel had been blocked by dirt. That crafty, sly old fox!

Obaku – The Eater of Dreams

Evil dreams are caused by evil spirits. Such dreams can include two snakes together, a fox with the voice of a man, bloodstained garments, a talking rice pot, or other such curiosities. You can ask an *obaku* to devour the dream for you, or you can have a picture of an *obaku* on your wall or write his name on your pillow. The creature has the face of a lion, the body of a horse, the tail of a crow, a rhino's horn and the feet of a tiger.

The Tradition of Cancelling Each Other Out

It is said that the snake, the toad and the snail cancel each other out. The idea is that there needs to be a power check in place. It works like this: the snake will eat the toad, but the toad has eaten a snail so that when the snake digests the toad, the snail (which is considered poisonous to a snake), kills the serpent. Therefore, the snake does not eat the toad as he knows it will kill him in the end.

The Fox Dream

One night a fisherman was working very late, past midnight, and while packing away his boat he saw his wife walking eerily along the beach in the sand. Knowing that his wife would never leave the house at this time, he considered the vision to be a fox. Taking his knife, he crept up behind the 'wife', stabbed her and cut her throat. She fell down dead. Looking down and expecting to find a transformed fox, he simply saw the body of his dead wife. Panic set in. She should have changed back into a fox! Running home, he was pleased to find his wife still asleep and so woke her. On waking she said that she had dreamt she was forced into action by a fox. The fisherman went back to the site of his deed and found that it had turned into a fox at last – all was well.

The Fox with Its Head Stuck

A traveller was walking through a village at night and needed shelter. He saw one lit house, and asked to be taken in. The occupant was glad and said that he was welcome because a woman had just died and the man needed to fetch some things. He therefore asked if the traveller would look after the body while he was away. Desperate, the traveller said yes and waited in the next room to the old dead woman. During the night, the traveller heard something and looked through the paper screen to the light beyond; the dead lady sat upright. Scared but with his wits still intact, he took a closer look. There in the corner of the room was the head of a fox, coming through the side of the wall. He went around the back of the house and, sure enough, the fox had its head stuck in the wall through a small hole. The traveller picked up a log and beat the fox to death, which brought an end to the matter.

Tokutaro and the Fox Bet

Tokutaro did not believe in the power of foxes, and so his friends made a wager with him challenging him to stay on the moor overnight. He agreed, journeying to the moor in the dark. He had not been there long when a fox crossed his path, but it disappeared out of sight. At this point a girl came from the darkness, saying that she was visiting her parents nearby and that he should go with her as a guide. Fully suspicious that it may be the power of the fox, he followed behind. When they got to the house, the family were surprised to see their daughter away from her husband. Tokutaro said that it was not their daughter but a fox-witch. He made them leave the room, where he beat and tortured the girl. As she would not confess to being a fox he burnt her alive, at which point the family rushed in and restrained him. A priest came by and asked the family to spare him so that he may become a priest for the remainder of his life. Tokutaro, happy at not being arrested for murder, agreed and let the priest shave his head. However, the priest and the house disappeared; it had all been an illusion. Tokutaro sat there with a shaved head. The foxes had tricked him, and he lost the bet.

The Kind Fox
One day a man was walking along a road when he came upon some boys tormenting a fox cub. The man saved the fox cub from the boys and let it return to its family. The man actually had a son who was very ill, and the only remedy was the liver of a live fox. Later, a stranger came to the door and said he had found the man a fox liver, and the boy was cured. The next day a woman appeared, and said that she was the fox cub's mother. She said that she knew of his need to save his own child, so out of compassion for his kindness she had removed the liver from her own cub and had her husband bring it to him.

The Hunter and the Demon Priest
A hunter sat under a large tree at night when on a trip in the mountains. He had set up holy ropes to protect himself from evil, and he had loaded his musket and set it across his chest. During the night he woke to the sound of a great flapping, and

above him was a demonic priest with a cape of scarlet. The demon could not pass the barrier of the holy rope, although thrice that night he tried.

The Wife and Her Horse Husband

There was a man who had only a daughter and a horse. The daughter loved the horse very much, and announced that it was to be her husband. The father, horrified, took the horse to the woods and hanged it from a tree. The girl was distraught when she discovered this and ran to the hanging horse in tears, clinging to it. The father cut the head off the horse, at which point his daughter turned into a white goddess and flew away. The branch that the horse was hung from was cut into three sections, and a figure of the goddess was carved in each one. It is said that at least one of those figurines remains in the village to this day.

Tengu Hill

Once a man went up *Tengu* Hill and met a stranger with whom he wrestled – the stranger being truly strange in that he was too tall to be Japanese. The stranger knocked the man out and left him there. Months later, the same man went back up the hill and never returned. The villagers later found his body ripped to shreds.

The Fool of Fire

Yoshiko was a village fool who wandered from house to house. She used to pick up wood and smell it, turning it in her hands, giving it her full concentration. From time to time she would throw a stone or block of wood at a nearby house and shout, 'Fire!' Then, without doubt, days or weeks later the house would catch fire. Noticing this, the villagers began to protect their homes from Yoshiko. However, every house touched in this way by

Yoshiko burned down. The question remains, was this Yoshiko's talent to predict or to curse?

Fukuji's Wife

Fukuji was a man who had lost his wife and son in a tidal wave. One night in the fog he saw two figures, one his wife and the other her first and true love. Fukuji talked with his wife, pleading for her to return from the dead to see their remaining children. She refused, and the dead lovers returned to the mist. After this conversation, Fukuji was ill due to his encounter with the dead.

Mountain Mother

Yamahaha is a mountain hag and may be close to other versions of mountain demons. In Tono she is called mother-mountain, but she seems to be supernatural in her powers and is akin to the wicked old hag of Western fairy stories. Below are two stories of Yamahaha.

I

One day a girl's parents leave her at home, and in classic fairy tale style they tell her not to open the door to anyone. Of course, a few hours later there is a knocking at the door and there is old Yamahaha. The girl refuses her entrance, but the hag says she will break down the door so the girl reluctantly lets her in. The old crone shouts for food; the child makes it and then flees as fast as she can. At first she hides with a woodcutter behind a stack of wood, but Yamahaha smells her out; again she flees, but this time she ends up in a reed field. Again she is discovered. In her escape she finds a pond and hides in a tree above it. Yamahaha smells the air and sees the reflection of the girl in the pond and jumps in, thinking it is her. The girl flees once more and comes to a bamboo hut where another girl is sitting. Giving advice, the girl in the hut tells the escapee to climb into a stone chest. In bursts Yamahaha, asking where the runaway girl is, but the girl in the hut says she is not there. Yamahaha says she can smell human flesh and that she is lying. The girl responds by saying she has just cooked a sparrow and that's what she can smell. Yamahaha, getting sleepy, says that she will rest a while and wonders if she should sleep in the stone chest or the wooden chest. The girl says that the wooden chest is warmer, and so Yamahaha gets into that chest. At this point both girls plan their escape. The girls lock up the wooden chest, burn holes in it and pour a vat of boiling water though them to kill the old witch.

II

A girl is soon to be married, and her parents go to town to buy things for the wedding. They tell her not to answer the door until they return. Yamahaha breaks into the house, kills the girl and butchers her corpse, eating her flesh and wearing the skin to disguise herself as the daughter with her mountain magic. The parents return to find their 'daughter' unharmed, dutifully waiting for them. They show her all the gifts they have bought, but in the yard a cockerel cries, 'That's not your daughter, look in the corner, cock a doodle do.' The parents, perplexed, ignore the strange event. They put her on a horse to leave for the wedding, but the cockerel cries again, 'That's not your daughter, that's Yamahaha, cock a doodle do.' The parents drag their 'daughter' from the horse and beat her to death. They investigate the corner as the cockerel advised and they find a pile of bones, the remains of their true daughter.

14

GAMES AND GHOST STORIES

Japanese games, whether for men, women, children or just for drinking, encompass such a large area. This is just a quick glance at the darker side of such pastimes, but it does give an idea of the haunting and ghostly games that were once popular in the land of Japan.

Hyakumonogatari Kaidankai – One Hundred Haunted Poems

A group of people will sit in a single room with one hundred candles or lamps with one hundred wicks. They take it in turns to tell a poem about a ghost or some other scary subject, normally only a few lines long. After each poem one of the candles is snuffed out, making the room grow darker as the tension builds and the stories reach a climax. At the telling of the hundredth poem, the last wick is put out and it is said that a real ghost will appear and that the players should all cry out in a ghostly fashion.

Kon Dame Shi – The Game of Soul Examining

In what is probably the most terrifying children's game of all time, the players (or hardcore thrillseekers) place flags or strips of cloth in the most horrible, dark and haunted place they can – for example, a graveyard, a haunted wood or an abandoned house – and in the dark they tell each other scary stories. After each story is told, a single player has to venture deep into the haunted area and retrieve one of the flags. This is done until there are no flags left or no one wishes to go in and fetch them.

Obake – The Ghost

In this child's game, a person will let down their long hair and brush it in front of their face and cross their eyes in what is a classic Japanese ghost image. They will then hold their arms outstretched in zombie fashion and cry like a ghost, chasing the other children in a game similar to Tag. Remember, *obake* is the more humorous and 'childish' form of the word for 'spectre'.

Kokkuri – 'Is Anybody There?'

Take three bamboo sticks and form a tripod, then place a wooden dish or plate on top of the tripod with a bowl of rice in the centre of that. The participants sit around this construction with their fingers lightly touching the wooden plate. They chant the words 'Kokkuri-sama, Kokkuri-sama, please descend, please descend, please descend quickly.' Do this for about ten minutes, and then ask if the spirit has come. If it has, ask it to show this by tilting the stand towards one of the people. Questions are then asked; the spirits can answer *yes* by lifting the leg and *no* by remaining still. It is also interesting that the name Kokkuri is of unknown origin, but the most common ideograms used to spell out the name are 'fox' (*ko*), 'dog' (*ku*, not *inu* due to its position) and 'racoon-dog' (*ri*) – which of course are three of the more famous monsters in the supernatural world. It is thought that this game was actually introduced by American sailors in the late 1800s and that the Japanese gave it their own name as they could not pronounce the English name.

15

SUPERSTITIONS IN MODERN JAPAN

This book has been full of legends and myths and old stories, so it seems fitting to conclude with a small selection of superstitions that have made it into modern times and illustrate how the themes and stories discussed have left their mark upon the modern Japanese mind. While the modern world is taking the mystery of out Japan and leaving behind a neon world of business, it is comforting to know that a small trail of weirdness has been left behind in things like anime and Japanese horror films, and also in the following ideas.

You should not kill a spider in the morning, but instead kill it at night. This is done because a spider in the morning brings good luck whereas a spider at night is a thief, someone who infiltrates. Also, a spider in the morning is a messenger from Heaven, while a spider at night is a messenger from Hell.

If a cat washes its face then it is going to rain.

Do not remove navel fluff; if you do you will get stomach ache.

If you cut your nails at night, you will die before your parents. This may be because night (夜) and nail (爪) together is pronounced '*yozume*', which is the same as 世詰, which means 'to shorten life'.

If you whistle at night, a snake, ghost or monster will appear before you.

If you want to grow more hair, you should eat *wakame* and *konbu* seaweed.

If you play with fire at night, you will wet your bed.

A woman who is born in the year *hinoe-uma* (one of a sixty-year cycle according to the old Chinese calendar) is a great worry for the family. The supposed problem with women born in this year is due to '*hinoe*' being associated with the fire element and the resulting implication that a wife born in the year has the stubbornness of a horse and a fiery temper; it is even said she may kill her own husband. This idea comes from the famous Edo period story 'The Greengrocer's Daughter' (mentioned earlier), where in 1681 the titular daughter, Oshichi, fell in love with a man as she was taking refuge from a fire. She thought she could meet him again if there was a fire in the town and so she started another fire; at this time she was supposedly sixteen years old, being born in the year of *hinoe-uma* in 1666. This story was often used in books and plays and has resulted in people trying to avoid having a daughter who is born in the year *hinoe-uma*. According to the Japanese Ministry of Health, Labour and Welfare (Kosei Rodo Sho), the Japanese birth rate dropped by 25 per cent in 1966, the last occurrence of *hinoe-uma*. The next year of *hinoe-uma* is in 2026, so it remains to be seen if the same thing will happen.

A wife who is bossy in her family tends to have a boy, while if the husband is bossy the wife tends to have a girl.

It is considered bad manners to stick your chopsticks into your rice in an upright position. This is because it mimics a part of the funeral rite when dealing with the ashes of the dead.

If you are in the middle of three in a photograph you will die earlier than the other two people.

If you do not put dolls away after the Girls' Festival (3 March in modern Japan), you will not get married or will get married late.

When serving fish, the head must point to the left or it is unlucky.

It is a sign of good luck to have a tea stalk floating erect in your tea; however, if you tell someone, your luck will flee.

Do not give a potted plant to someone who is in the hospital or who is sick. People do not like it because 'potted plant' in Japanese means 'take root', which also means 'stay in bed longer'. Also, the Japanese do not choose the camellia flower when visiting people. Camellia is not favoured because when the petals fall they often fall as a complete head, which is reminiscent of the decapitated head of a human and therefore associated with the beheading of a criminal.

The Japanese consider odd numbers as lucky and even numbers as unlucky based on the idea of *yin-yang* (positive and negative). When giving someone celebratory gift money or obituary gift money, people choose amounts with the numbers one, three or five, for example: ¥3,000 (three notes of ¥1,000); ¥5,000 (five notes of ¥1,000); ¥10,000 (one note of ¥10,000); ¥30,000 (three notes of ¥10,000); ¥50,000 (five notes of ¥10,000). They never choose the numbers four or nine, for the reasons discussed earlier (see the Numbers section in chapter 13).

The *shikii* (threshold), the wooden rails that *shoji* (sliding doors) and *fusuma* (panels) move along, must not be stood upon. This is bad manners because a god lives in the threshold, and if you step on them then your family will not prosper. The *shikii* can also be seen as a barrier between worlds, between inside and outside, and therefore if you step on it you break the barrier. Also, you should not step on the edge of a tatami mat.

When women are nineteen and thirty-three years old they visit shrines to get rid of evil because these years are considered malevolent. The same goes for men when they are twenty-five, forty-two and sixty years old (but remember that Japan used to start counting lifespans at one, so it will be the year before for each of the above in the West). See photo overleaf.

If you urinate onto an earthworm (also a slug), your penis will swell (get digging, boys!).

If you talk to someone who is talking in his sleep they will die young.

If your sandal string snaps, your teacup breaks or a picture frame falls by itself, something bad will happen soon.

やく年

	男性		女性	
	数え歳	生まれ年	生まれ年	数え歳
前厄	41才	48年生まれ	57年生まれ	32才
大厄	42才	47年生まれ	56年生まれ	33才
後厄	43才	46年生まれ	55年生まれ	34才
中厄	25才	平成元年生まれ	平成7年生まれ	19才
還暦	61才	28年生まれ		61才

Do not do needlework before you go out of the house.

Wear new shoes for the first time before sunset. However, if you have to wear shoes after sunset, you should put charcoal on the soles.

Yo-me and *to-me* is a warning not to date people four or ten years younger or older than you as it is bad luck.

If you place a hand mirror with the mirror side upwards then evil things will come to you.

When pregnant women attend funerals they should put a mirror near their belly – probably inside their clothes.

In modern Japan, a pregnant woman will wear a white cotton *obi* belt on the Day of the Dog in her fifth month of pregnancy. Then she will pray for an easy delivery, like that of a dog.

If you leave grains of rice in a bowl after a meal, you will lose your sight.

If a swallow flies low, it will rain.

Cover your navel when it thunders because the god of thunder will take your navel (remember the crazy story from before where he wants to eat them).

When a child loses its first teeth, throw the bottom teeth on to the roof and throw the upper teeth under the floor into the space between the ground and the house.

If you tell a lie, the Regent of Hell will pull your tongue out.

If you sleep or lie down as soon as you finish a meal, you will turn into a cow.

CONCLUSION
PUTTING THE MAGIC BACK IN JAPAN

It is my hope that you will no longer see Japan as a domain of the salaryman but instead as a realm where the stories and customs of the past have been imbued with new life. Where once there were stacks of flat-screen televisions, now visualise clusters of moss-covered gravestones; where once you saw the bullet train, envision the passage to the underworld; and where once you saw capsule hotels, visualise the realm of the gods and the vast magic of the stars.

It cannot be said that Japanese culture is greater or lesser than any other world culture, but what makes it distinct is that it was untouched by the modern world for so long; indeed, it was only a few generations ago that its medieval period faded from living memory. The strong echo of that time has only begun to die in the last few decades, and before it falls silent it is our task to capture it.

The inevitability of the loss of Japanese customs is certain, as no nation in the world remains untouched by our pervasive new global culture. While our move towards the future is achieved at different rates in different countries, we are all moving towards a single global community with a single world culture, and slowly but surely the old world is fading. The reason we must try to capture as much of the zest of old Japan – and indeed of all customs of the past – is because without known truths, the media will reinvent history for us. For newer generations, popular history is taught through film, TV and comics. In itself this is a good thing, for without them history would not exist for the youth. But why not give them real history through those media avenues? Why not demonstrate that *true* history is far more exciting than invented history?

Your journey into Japanese folklore and magic is not at an end, as only the dark side has been covered here. There is still that which is curious and that which is heavenly, and they, with this volume, form a snapshot of a land before our time which supported a culture that was truly magical.

SELECT BIBLIOGRAPHY

Aston, W. G., *Shinto: The Way of the Gods* (Longmans, 1905)

Blacker, C., 'Animal Witchcraft in Japan' in *The Witch Figure* (London: Routledge, 1973)

Blacker, C., *The Catalpa Bow* (George & Allen, 1975)

Blacker, C., *The Collected Writings of Carmen Blacker* (Surrey: Japan Library, 2000)

Byron Earheart, H., *A Religious Study of the Mount Haguro Sect of Shugendo* (Tokyo: Sophia University, 1970)

Cummins and Minami, *The True Path of the Ninja* (Vermont, Tuttle Publishing, 2011)

Ekiken, K. and Wilson, W. S. (trans.), *Yojokun* (Tokyo: Kodansha Publishing, 2008)

Etter, C., *Aborigines of Japan* (Wilcox & Follet Company, 1949)

Foster, M., *Pandemonium and Parade: Japanese Monsters and the Culture of Yokai* (London: University of California Press, 2009)

Hadland-Davies, F., *Myths & Legends of Japan* (London: George G. Harrap & Company, 1912)

Hori, I., *Folk Religion In Japan* (London: University of Chicago Press, 1968)

Lane, J., *Legend in Japanese Art* (New York: John Lane Company, 1908)

Mitford, A. B., *Tales of Old Japan* (London: Macmillan and Co., 1874)

Mol, S., *Invisible Armour: An Introduction to the Esoteric Dimension of Japan's Classical Warrior Arts* (Belgium: Eibusha Press, 2008)

More, R. A., *Legends of Tono* (Tokyo: The Japan Foundation, 1975)

Otake R., *Katori Shinto Ryu: Warrior Tradition* (New Jersey: Koryu Books, 2009)

Rankin, A., *Seppuku: A History of Samurai Suicide* (New York: Kodansha International, 2011)

Philip, N., *The Illustrated Book of Myths* (London: Dorling Kindersley, 1995)

Picken, S. D. B., *Sourcebook in Shinto* (Westport: Preager Publishing, 2004)

Rokkum, A., *Nature, Ritual and Society in Japan's Ryukyu Islands* (New York: Routledge, 2006)

Ryerson, E., *The Netsuke of Japan: Illustrating Legends, History, Folklore & Customs* (London: C. Bell & Sons Ltd, 1958)

Sasaki, H., *Jujutsu no Hon* (Tokyo: Gakushu Kenkyusha Publishing, 2003)

Seward, J., *Hara-kiri: Japanese Ritual Suicide* (Vermont: Tuttle Publishing, 1968)

Stevens, J., *The Marathon Monks of Mount Hiei* (Boston: Shambhala Publishing, 1988)

Toyoshima, Y., *Zusetsu Nihon Jujutsu Zensho* (Tokyo: Harashobo Books, 1998)

Yamakage, M., *The Essence of Shinto* (Tokyo: Kodansha, 2006)

Waterhouse, D., 'Notes on Kuji' in Kornicki & McMullen, *Religion in Japan* (New York: Cambridge University Press, 1996)

ABOUT THE AUTHOR & ILLUSTRATOR

Antony Cummins heads the Historical Ninjutsu Research Team, a project that documents, translates and publishes medieval documents pertaining to the *shinobi* of Japan. Alongside this, Antony has revived an old samurai school of war, Natori-Ryu, with the aim of educating people on historical Japanese warfare. He would like to establish a correct understanding of Japanese military arts and to bring about a deeper understanding and respect for them. He is on most social media and information can be found at www.natori.co.uk.

David Osborne lives in the Blue Ridge Mountains of North Carolina in the United States. He is a full-time criminal investigator for a police department where he supervises a unit of detectives. He is also a North Carolina certified instructor in police arrest and control concepts. David has trained in a variety of traditional martial arts systems during his life and has a diverse background of study. His primary focus has been in Samurai Aiki-jujutsu and more recently in modern systems such as Krav Maga. His years of study and personal research in martial arts have led him to create a new system of Goshin Jutsu under the school name of Yamakage Ryu. As a student of Natori Ryu, he follows the historical research and work of Antony Cummins and facilitates a study group of Natori Ryu teachings in his area.

Images on following two pages courtesy of the Library of Congress and Rijksmuseum

郵便報知新聞

第六百二十三号

信州水内郡野尻駅の木賃物屋の重吉が明里
用事ありて重詰の旅飯料拵抔を調家
の女を倶されて出て午自の鴬合三人の
旅客来り宿を求めて夜食を持せられ
之を握り焼になし差出し之より夫
れ炉辺に持来り囲炉裡の湯を入るよう
祇遊を奉る杉大に疑ひ客家の雷箱に
穴口と荷物を扱らせ我妻并に隣の女
々衣類遣入る撰ひ廻賊へ入りなり近辺
壮者を集め二人を縛り仔細を糾せば
沢間ぞて追剥二人共立木に話り置
ごと白状され二人へ松火をうつし
かく夜明る彼所に至りそれ処の婚をり
而して赤裸にて立木に縛られ
て骨をどろ肉を狼の為に喰とられ
ごと